Sea Survival Handbook

The Complete Guide to Survival at Sea
by Keith Colwell

Foreword by Mike Golding
Illustrations by Steve Lucas

Skyhorse Publishing books may be purchased in bulk at special discounts for sales promotion, corporate gifts, fund-raising, or educational purposes. Special editions can also be created to specifications. For details, contact the Special Sales Department, Skyhorse Publishing, 555 Eighth Avenue, Suite 903, New York, NY 10018 or info@skyhorsepublishing.com.

www.skyhorsepublishing.com

10 9 8 7 6 5 4 3 2 1

Library of Congress Cataloging-in-Publication Data

Colwell, Keith.
  Sea survival handbook : the complete guide to survival at sea / Keith Colwell.
     p. cm.
  Includes index.
  ISBN 978-1-60239-695-1
  1. Survival after airplane accidents, shipwrecks, etc.--Handbooks,
manuals, etc. 2. Boats and boating--Safety measures--Handbooks, manuals,
etc. 3. Boating accidents--Handbooks, manuals, etc. I. Title.
  VK1259.C655 2009
  613.6'909162--dc22
                                        2009008928

Printed in China

Acknowledgments: Ralph Macdonald Boatswain Joint Services Adventurous Sail Training Center, Steve Judkins JSASTC.
Cover Design: Design House
Illustrations: Steve Lucas
Typeset: Creativebyte
Proofreading, index, and glossary: Alan Thatcher

Contents

Foreword
By Mike Golding

"Sea Survival training saves lives, it is essential knowledge for the modern offshore skipper. The stark fact is, if things do go dramatically wrong onboard, this knowledge can save lives. Training for the worst eventuality will make you better prepared and it will give you the confidence to know that you have planned for every conceivable circumstance when you leave port. The sea can be a hostile and brutal place for the ill prepared, you don't need to be in the Southern Ocean, the English Channel or anywhere away from easy access to shore, can quickly become just as dangerous and hostile if things go badly wrong onboard your boat. When it comes to survival, preparation is everything and all good preparation begins with solid information and sound practical training.

This book highlights the importance of having the correct safety equipment and will also give you the knowledge of know how and when to use it. Armed with this information and the right equipment every eventuality onboard, no matter how severe, can be met with the determination and conviction that is the essential mark of every survivor."

Introduction

Boating is one of the safest leisure sporting activities. However, in any sport that pushes us to the edge of our abilities, there's always a chance of accident or injury. Being properly prepared makes us better able to cope with an emergency and will significantly increase our chances of survival.

This handbook is essential for anyone taking the one-day RYA Basic Sea Survival course and the two-day RYA/ISAF Offshore Safety course. It is also invaluable for anyone who takes a boat offshore.

K. Colwell

For further information and a list of establishments running RYA Training Courses, contact the RYA at RYA House, Ensign Way, Hamble, Southampton, SO31 4YA. Tel 0845 345 0400 Fax 0845 345 0329

CHAPTER 1 : Before you go out

Check the weather forecast and tides. Familiarize yourself with the area you're planning to sail. Are you and your crew sufficiently skilled for the planned trip? Tell somebody ashore where you are planning to go, when you expect to get there and how many people are on board. Let them know when you expect to arrive and what to do if you don't contact them to tell them of your safe arrival.

Many other countries have similar voluntary or compulsory registration schemes, so check if the country in which you keep your boat has a scheme and how you can join.

Safety brief

As skipper you should ensure that everyone on board knows where the safety equipment is stowed and how to use it. Talk them through your passage and pilotage as well as your contingency plan should something go wrong. Don't forget the less obvious safety equipment and procedures such as how to drop anchor or how to read your current position off the GPS or chart.

Are your crew familiar with boating? Is there anything you should know about them? Can they swim? Do they have medical problems that you need to be aware of, such as asthma, diabetes or angina? As skipper, their safety is your responsibility.

Safety brief checklist

Lifejackets _____Check condition, lights, when and how to don and inflate

Harnesses _____When and where to clip on

Flares _____Where stowed and how to fire

Liferaft _____Where stowed and how to launch and inflate

Grab bag _____Where it is, also other items such as water, food, etc.

Onboard hazards _____Boom, winches, cleats, ropes, etc.

Anchoring procedure

How to start the engine

Lifebuoy/dan buoy

VHF radio _____Mayday and DSC procedures

GPS _____How to read off a position

Bilge pump _____Where and how to use it

First-aid kit _____Where it is kept

Fire extinguishers _____Where, what type, and how to use them

Medicines _____Are they taking any medication including anti-seasickness tablets

Clothing _____Spare clothing, sunscreen

Lookout _____Tell me what you see and hear; I may not have seen or heard it!

Passage Plan _____Where we are going and contingency plans

MOB recovery equipment ____Where and how to use it

Watch rota _____When to call the skipper

Can they swim?

Medical or physical problems?

VHF tip

Operating procedures for marine-band radios vary from set to set. Stick a prompt-card in a prominent position close to the set. Make sure the crew know not only how to switch on the radio—including the correct switch on the distribution board—but also how to use the DSC distress button (if fitted) and how to choose Ch 16 and transmit a Mayday.

Your MMSI number and call sign should be prominently displayed beside the radio.

Clear labels on lockers and a plan of where the safety equipment is stowed will save time and help reduce panic during an emergency. Place a copy on the door in the heads, where crew may find the time to study it!

Labelling will assist SAR (Search and Rescue) crew if they need to come aboard during a rescue.

Make a plan

Think about what can go wrong and how you can reduce the severity of an incident.

For example, ask yourself:

- What would you do in a range of emergencies?
- How would you go about abandoning ship?
- What you would do if somebody went overboard and how would you recover them?
- When should you fire flares or make a Mayday call?
- What is your contingency plan?
- Talk your procedures through and, where possible, practice them with your crew.

Clothing

Do you have the right clothing for the conditions? Take extra and spare clothing with you because conditions at sea are more hostile than on land.

Synthetic materials are better at wicking moisture away from the skin. Breathable waterproofs keep you warmer not only by keeping you dry from the outside but also by preventing moisture created by your body from becoming trapped inside the clothing.

Most marine clothing manufacturers now provide layer systems that are better at keeping you comfortable in a range of weather conditions.

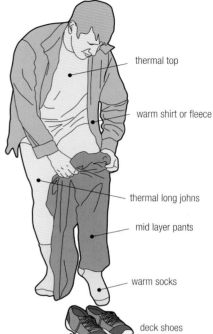

thermal top

warm shirt or fleece

thermal long johns

mid layer pants

warm socks

deck shoes

Cool weather clothing

woolly or fleece hat

reflective tape on hood

good neck seal

gas inflation lifejacket with harness

waterproof jacket

non-release harness clip

tight seal around wrists

sailing gloves for handling ropes

lifejacket crotch strap(s)

harness line

hi-fit waterproof trousers

good ankle seal

waterproof non-slip boots

Warm weather clothing

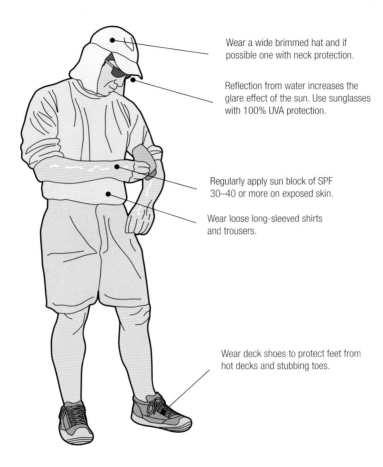

Wear a wide brimmed hat and if possible one with neck protection.

Reflection from water increases the glare effect of the sun. Use sunglasses with 100% UVA protection.

Regularly apply sun block of SPF 30–40 or more on exposed skin.

Wear loose long-sleeved shirts and trousers.

Wear deck shoes to protect feet from hot decks and stubbing toes.

In hot weather, protect yourself from the sun. UV light is reflected by the sea and will increase the possibility of sunburn. Use sun block or high-factor cream. Don't forget vulnerable areas such as tops of your feet, ears and the front of your legs. Long-sleeved shirts and broad-brimmed hats give added protection and wrap-around sunglasses reduce glare.

Recommended safety equipment for sailing yachts

The amount of safety gear you carry depends mainly on where you are planning to sail. Here's a selection of recommended equipment.

Before you start your voyage, leave details with a shore contact. Check requirements for all the countries you are sailing.

Comprehensive first aid kit and sufficient knowledge to use it correctly

Fire blanket near, but not over cooker

Serviced fire extinguisher for each accommodation space

Enough fuel and water for the passage plus an adequate reserve

Snap shackle on bottom of main sheet for MOB rescue

System to washboard place in the e of capsize

Lifejackets with lights, crotch straps and spray hoods, spares and rearming kits, harnesses, and wet weather gear for all the crew

Fog horn

Try to keep the port quarter clear for helecopter rescue

Dan buoy attached to lifebuoy

Accurate main and hand bearing compasses

Emergency steering

Floating rescue line

Lifebuoy, floating light, and drogue

Powerful spotlight and torch with spare batteries and bulbs

Two buckets with lanyards and a hand bilge pump for use in awkward spaces

Dinghy with oars, repair kit, pump, anchor, engine with fuel, tools, and kill cord

Comprehensive tool kit including sail repair kit, spare navigation l bulbs, and fuses

Spare battery ca

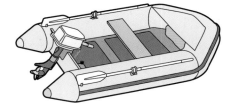

Fully serviced engine, with handbook, adequate spares, and sufficient knowledge to effect repairs

Gas kept in a properly vented locker with all pipes and connections regularly checked for leaks

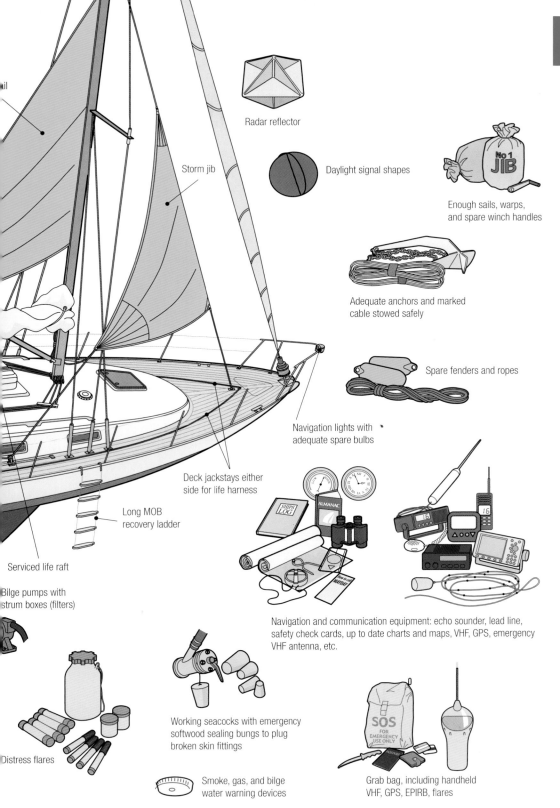

il

Radar reflector

Storm jib

Daylight signal shapes

Enough sails, warps,
and spare winch handles

Adequate anchors and marked
cable stowed safely

Spare fenders and ropes

Navigation lights with
adequate spare bulbs

Deck jackstays either
side for life harness

Long MOB
recovery ladder

Serviced life raft

Bilge pumps with
strum boxes (filters)

Navigation and communication equipment: echo sounder, lead line,
safety check cards, up to date charts and maps, VHF, GPS, emergency
VHF antenna, etc.

Working seacocks with emergency
softwood sealing bungs to plug
broken skin fittings

Distress flares

Smoke, gas, and bilge
water warning devices

Grab bag, including handheld
VHF, GPS, EPIRB, flares

Equipment for motorboats

Mechanical failure is the main cause of problems in a motorboat. Ensure engines are regularly serviced and checked. Carry sufficient fuel for the proposed voyage. One of the main causes of crew accidents on a motorboat is the helmsman making a sudden maneuver without informing the rest of the crew, who can be thrown off their feet (or worse overboard). While motorboats will carry much of the same equipment as sailing boats, the lack of rigging and the dependence on mechanical power can bring specific problems.

Adequate anchors and marked cable stowed safely

Spare fenders and ropes

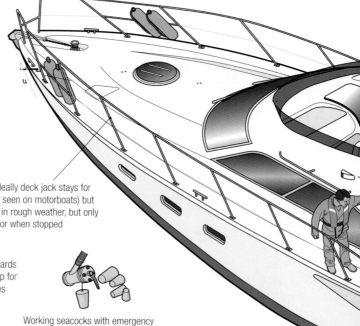

Proper height deck rails and ideally deck jack stays for a life harness (these are rarely seen on motorboats) but would be quite useful on deck in rough weather, but only when traveling at slow speed, or when stopped

Two buckets with lanyards and a hand bilge pump for use in awkward spaces

Working seacocks with emergency softwood sealing bungs to plug broken skin fittings or broken pipework

Automatic fire extinguishers

Well secured battery banks as they can be quite large on motorboats. They also need to be properly ventilated, maintained and monitored

Spare battery capacity

Comprehensive tool kit including spare engine parts, spare navigation light bulbs, and fuses

Bilge pumps are important on a motorboat since a high-speed collision can cause the boat to become inundated very quickly. Large battery banks and plenty of power to recharge them allow electric pumps to be fitted but do not forget to add manual pump as a backup, in case the electric pump fails

Engines and all other related systems need to have sensing devices to warn well in advance if anything is going wrong. Fuel should be able to be isolated in the event of an emergency with the use of on/off fuel taps in fuel lines

Smoke, gas and bilge water warning devices

Fire blanket near, but not over cooker

FIRE BLANKET

Fully serviced fire extinguisher for each accommodation space

Grab bag with handheld VHF, GPS, EPIRB, flares

Radar reflector

Powerful searchlight to help with coming into harbor or picking up a buoy at night—and poor visibility MOB rescue

Distress flares

SOS FOR EMERGENCY USE ONLY

Powerful foghorn

Navigation lights with adequate spare bulbs

Floating rescue line

Comprehensive first aid kit and sufficient knowledge to use it correctly

Deck floodlight

MOB danbuoy (rarely seen on motorboats)

Horseshoe lifebuoy, floating light, and drogue

Lifejackets with lights, crotch straps, and spray hoods for everyone on board, sufficient suitable rearming kits

Liferaft with hydrostatic release as motorboats can go down very quickly if anything is hit at speed. Regularly checked and maintained

Tender and outboard properly maintained, regularly checked with sufficient fuel

FIREFLY

Sufficient fuel and water for the passage plus an adequate reserve

Gas bottles to be installed in a properly vented locker, also make sure all the pipework and connections are checked for leaks on a regular basis

Appropriate navigation and communication equipment: echo sounder, lead line, safety check cards, up-to-date charts, h/h and fixed VHF, binoculars, torch, etc.

Immersion (Survival) suits

Not usually found aboard most cruising yachts, although increasing in popularity with professional yachtsmen and commercial small boat operators, the cold water immersion suit has been designed for larger commercial craft.

Since July 2006, an immersion suit is required for every person on board a cargo vessel that operates in a cold-water area. They are often bulky which is not conductive to easy stowage aboard a small yacht.

There are a broad variety of types from thick neoprene insulated suits to those that are made from PU-coated nylon which are similar to diving or watersports drysuits and require insulated clothing to be worn beneath the suit. Both types usually have insulated hoods to minimize heat loss from the head.

They require practice to be donned quickly.

Unless built-in buoyancy is provided, a 275N lifejacket (see p.33) must be worn to ensure sufficient buoyancy to turn and keep the immersion suit wearer face up.

Donning an immersion suit

Care and maintenance of boat and equipment

For the safe operation of a boat at sea, it's essential to inspect and regularly service not only safety equipment but also the boat's machinery, structure, and systems. The smallest failure can sometimes be the beginning of a catalogue of problems that can lead to a catastrophe. Prevention is far better than cure.

Follow the example of aircraft pilots—check your boat before departure and put right any problems:

- Do you have enough fuel?
- Does the engine have sufficient oil and water?
- Is the engine's raw-water filter clear of debris?
- Is there water or dirt in the fuel filter/water separator?
- Are the engine mounts secure?
- Is there water or oil or fuel in the bilge? If so investigate where it came from.
- Are the hoses securely clipped to the skin fittings?
- Are the seacocks working smoothly, and are softwood bungs fastened to them in case the skin fitting fractures?
- Is the steering free from stiffness or excessive play?
- Are the bilge pumps operational?
- Are the strum boxes clear of rubbish?
- Are the rigging pins in place at shroud bases?
- Are the lifejackets operational?
- Are the jackstays secure?
- Are the fire extinguishers up to pressure?
- Is the anchor ready?
- Is the liferaft ready?
- Is the lifebuoy ready and the lifebuoy light working?
- Is the dan buoy in place with the flag concertinaed (rather than rolled) so that it deploys quickly?
- Is the handheld VHF charged? Spare charged batteries available?
- Is the fixed VHF working?
- Are all the navigational instruments working?
- Are in-date flares readily to hand?

Always carry sufficient spares on board—engine oil, fuel filters, drive belts, water pump impellers, hoses and spare fuses.

Replace any items in the first-aid kit that need replacing. Make sure you have replacement batteries for handheld kit and that you have the right tools on board.

On sailing boats:

- Check the mast for wear or damage.
- Are the spreaders in their sockets?
- Are the navigation lights working properly?
- Are there any loose halyards, damaged rigging wires, or bent fittings?

Check the engine instruments. Lift the engine-room and floor hatches and check that all's well. Look around the deck and up the mast. Is there anything becoming loose or that has moved into an unusual position? Listen for unusual noises—they can indicate the beginning of something going wrong.

Remember to continue to make regular checks while on passage.

When a skipper is familiar with their boat they are more likely to quickly notice if anything is amiss.

Keep a log of items that need longer-term maintenance, including the dates that equipment such as flares, fire extinguishers, lifejackets, and liferaft require servicing or replacing. Regularly check all safety equipment for signs of corrosion and wear and tear and make a note of anything that's likely to need replacing in the near future.

Many items of safety equipment are rarely if ever used. It's easy for them to be forgotten and neglected. However, regular maintenance, servicing and inspections are necessary to ensure the equipment works when you need it.

Engine servicing must not be neglected. Engine failure is one of the main reasons for yachts (power and sail) to founder.

Put the boat's name or call sign on all safety equipment and other items that can float free so it is easily identified if found by the SAR services.

Tip
Add retro-reflective tape to the lifebuoy and danbuoy so that they can be seen more easily at night.

CHAPTER 2 : Weather

Marine weather forecasts are widely available. They are broadcast on public and commercial radio and by coast radio stations, Navtex, the Internet and on Inmarsat.

Times for radio broadcasts are shown in an almanac or RYA Weather Forecasts (G5).

Shipping forecast terms

Gale = Average wind expected to be F8 or more
Strong-wind warning = Average wind expected to be F6 or F7

Timing from the time of issue of warning or forecast
Imminent = within 6 hours , Soon = within 6–12 hours, Later = more than 12 hours

---

Visibility

Good = greater than 5 miles, Moderate = between 2 and 5 miles, Poor = 1,000 meters to 2 miles, Fog = less than 1,000 meters.

Fair = No significant precipitation

Backing = wind changing in an anticlockwise direction

Veering = wind changing in a clockwise direction

General synopsis = How, when and where the weather systems are moving

Sea states: Smooth = wave height 0.2–0.5m, Slight = wave height 0.5 to 1m, Moderate = wave height 1.25–2.5m, Rough = wave height 2.5–4m, Very rough = wave height 4–6m.

Pressure and tendency

Steady = change less than 0.1mb in 3 hours

Rising or falling slowly = change 0.1–1.5mb in the last 3 hours

Rising or falling = change 1.6–3.5mb in the last 3 hours

Rising or falling quickly = change 3.6–6mb in the last 3 hours

Rising or falling very rapidly = change of more than 6mb in the last 3 hours

Now rising, now falling = change from rising or falling or vice versa in the last 3 hours

Typical depression

Strong-wind weather is usually determined by Atlantic depressions formed by low pressure. As a depression moves across the country, the warm front is caught by the cold front, creating an occluded front. The lower the pressure in the low, the stronger the winds.

Clouds give a good indication of the approaching weather. High-altitude cirrus clouds give an indication that a depression is approaching. As the warm front approaches, the cloud base descends and pressure falls. Rain becomes heavier with poor visibility, then lightens to drizzle.

Movement of depression

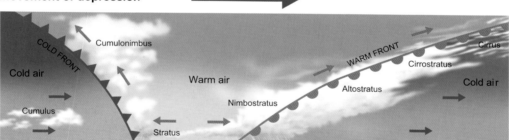

As the warm front passes, the wind veers and becomes steady and the air pressure settles. Visibility is moderate. Low-level fracto and altostratus cloud forms overhead.

A cold front approaches and the wind veers suddenly as the front passes over. Heavy rain, possibly hail and thunder may occur. Visibility is poor.

Behind a cold front, the pressure rises then levels. Sunshine and showers, visibility good except in showers. Cumulonimbus and then Cumulus clouds can be seen.

Local winds

Winds often vary from forecast due to local effects.

Wind is slowed by friction with the surface, which is greater over land than sea.

Wind blowing offshore can be variable in direction and strength, especially when blowing off trees, buildings, cliffs, valleys, etc.

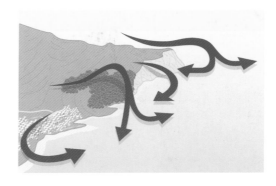

Wind backs more over land than sea. If the wind is blowing off the land, expect it to back as you approach the coast. This may affect the sea state depending on the direction of the tide.

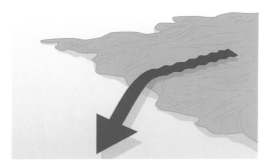

Fog
Advection or sea fog

Created when moist air blows over a colder sea. Usually associated, in the UK, with warm S or SW winds of a depression. Most common in spring when sea temperature is at its lowest.

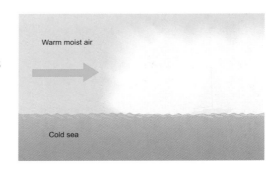

Warm moist air

Cold sea

Radiation or land fog

Occurs in settled weather in autumn/winter. Created when land cools quickly at night, causing moisture in the air to condense and form fog over land that will drift out to sea on a land breeze.

Beaufort scale

1 Light airs 1–3 knots
Ripples
Sail—drifting conditions
Power—fast, smooth planing conditions

2 Light breeze 4–6 knots
Small wavelets
Sail—full mainsail and large genoa
Power—fast planing conditions

3 Gentle breeze 7–10 knots
Occasional crests
Sail—full sail
Power—fast planing conditions

4 Moderate 11–16 knots
Frequent white horses
Sail—reduce headsail size
Power—fast but bumpy planing conditions

5 Fresh breeze 17–21 knots
Moderate waves, many white crests
Sail—reef mainsail
Power—reduce speed to prevent slamming
when going upwind

6 Strong breeze 22–27 knots

Large waves, white foam crests
Sail—reef main and reduce headsail
Power—displacement speed

7 Near gale 28–33 knots

Sea heaps up, spray, breaking waves, foam
blows in streaks
Sail—deep reefed main, small jib
Power—displacement speed

8 Gale 34–40 knots

Moderately high waves, breaking crests
Sail—deep reefed main, storm jib
Power—displacement speed, stern waves

9 Severe gale 41–47 knots

High waves, spray affects visibility
Sail—trysail and storm jib
Power—displacement speed, stern waves

10 Storm 48–55 knots

Very high waves, long breaking crests
Survival conditions

CHAPTER 3 : Preparing for heavy weather

Motorboats are less likely to find themselves caught in heavy weather since most have the speed and agility to find a safe haven quickly or, on longer passages, to route around a storm. Sailing yachts, however, often cannot avoid stormy conditions.

Whether under power or sail the following guidelines are a sensible precursor to heavy weather:

- Stow all gear securely
- Shut lockers and hatches
- Shut and secure portlights
- Stow essentials in plastic bags
- Turn off seacocks to toilet and sink
- Mark fix on chart and secure chart to table
- Update log
- Check contingency plans and, if not already done so, add appropriate waypoints to GPS
- Prepare contingency passage plans
- Sail away from the lee shore
- Print or write out weather forecast times and fasten to the chart area
- Organize a crew roster. Rest the strongest and most able crew first
- Eat a meal and prepare sandwiches and flasks of hot drinks
- Drink plenty of water
- Inform the Coastguard of your position and planned course
- Take anti-seasickness tablets
- Charge engine batteries
- Check bilges and ensure bilge pumps are working
- Check and wear safety equipment
- Secure cockpit lockers to prevent down-flooding
- Secure washboards in companionway
- If appropriate, shut watertight doors
- Stow loose items off deck
- Prepare and secure anchor locker
- Check sea anchor and heavy warps
- Rig and check jackstays
- Close off deck ventilators
- Check cockpit drains are clear
- If required, rig mainsail reefing pennant to third reef
- Prepare trysail and storm jib

Good seamanship—Prepared for heavy weather

Bad seamanship—Poorly stored gear after heavy weather

Shortening sail

As the wind strengthens you will need to shorten sail. Always shorten sail before you have to because it's easier to shake out a reef if the conditions allow than to take one in when the wind has increased.

The order of shortening sail will depend on your boat and rig. In general, the principle is to shorten sail by gradually reducing the headsail and mainsail so that the center of effort does not move too far forward or too far aft. This will keep the boat balanced and ensures sufficient weather helm is maintained.

Note that on some boats with slab or jiffy reefing only two reefing pennants are run. This requires the first reefing line to be reattached to the third or uppermost reefing cringle. Three reefs will reduce the mainsail by up to 60% of its total area.

While roller headsails can reduce sail area completely, a partially reefed roller headsail is very inefficient upwind and will not provide the proper balance.

Storm sails

If wind conditions increase, you will need to resort to storm sails comprising of a storm jib and trysail. These lower the center of effort and may help a yacht to be sailed off a lee shore. They are made from heavy-duty material usually colored bright-red or luminescent orange so that other shipping can more easily see the boat. A storm jib is best set on an inner forestay, this can be a rigged temporarily or permanently.

A trysail is a loose-footed sail. Its sheet is led aft either to a spinnaker pad eye or to a stern mooring cleat. Occasionally, it may be attached to the boom but this is not recommended.

Depending on type, a trysail can allow for the mainsail to be furled and secured to the boom. The boom can then be dropped and secured to the deck. A trysail can be hoisted in the mainsail's track or preferably in its own track. It must be securely fastened.

Both sails should be pre-rigged with their own sheets.

> Since the rigging of storm sails differs from that of ordinary sails, it's important to practice rigging them in fine weather rather than waiting until you really need them. Rig them in advance of a storm.

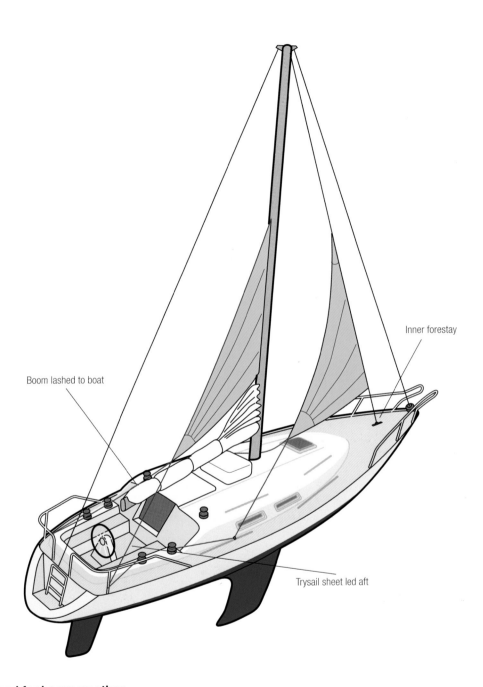

Inner forestay

Boom lashed to boat

Trysail sheet led aft

Rigged for heavy weather
Storm jib is best set on an inner forestay while the trysail replaces the mainsail.

Breaking waves

Waves are generated by the frictional effect of wind on the surface of the water. The stronger the wind, the longer it has blown and the greater the fetch (the distance to shelter from windward), the bigger the waves.

Very steep waves are formed when:
- the wind strength increases rapidly
- wind and current oppose each other—wind against tide
- waves are coming from different directions due to a sudden wind shift
- water becomes shallow

Waves break when they reach a critical steepness and gravity can no longer sustain their shape.

Compared to their size, breaking waves release enormous amounts of energy and they are often sufficient to knock down and capsize a boat.

When caught beam-on, a breaking wave the same height as the beam of the boat is enough to turn the boat upside down.

Owing to the boat's reduction in moment of inertia, a dismasted yacht is often more easily rolled by a breaking wave than one with a mast.

Avoid areas of breaking waves whenever possible.

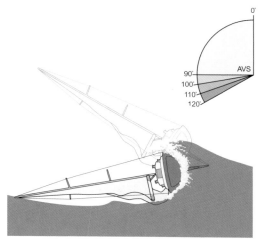

The Angle of Vanishing Stability will depend on the design of the boat. Many will not right themselves once inverted to 120°.

A breaking wave the same height as the beam can capsize the boat.

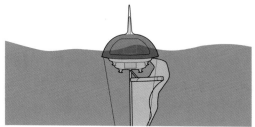

Many boats will stay upside down after capsizing.

CHAPTER 4 : Handling heavy weather

Your plan for handling heavy weather needs to take into account:

- capability of the boat
- capability of the crew
- severity of the expected weather conditions
- proximity to land

There are two basic strategies for handling heavy weather:

1. run for shelter
2. ride it out at sea

Running for shelter

Choose a haven that has a sheltered entrance, waves get bigger and steeper as they approach shallow water. An opposing tide will also increase wave size and steepness. Bigger waves travel faster and are more likely to break. When approaching a harbor entrance running with the waves, the increasing size of waves can be deceptive. Look behind you for waves catching you up. Good shelter and a wind with tide can make a flatter sea close in. Radio the Coastguard and harbor master for advice and to tell them of your intention.

Riding it out at sea

Riding it out at sea needs room. There are several methods:

Going to windward (sailing craft)
A good method in strong winds, but only if the crew are relatively strong, is to close reach across troughs, luff (steer) into and over crests and bear away hard to keep the leeward side in the water and avoid a slam. Keep steerage in the troughs or the yacht could end up beam-on to the next wave. Not a method to be used if the crew are tired, in darkness or strengthening winds.

Another option for yachts that do not behave well in stormy winds is to sail slowly upwind. Heavily reef the mainsail and set it as flat as possible and as tightly sheeted in as possible so that it acts as a stadying sail. The headsail is furled. A ketch or yawl would be better using the mizzen rather than the mainsail. Adjust the boat's speed so that it is just moving forward, speeding up to miss breaking waves.

Heaving to
Reduces strain on the yacht and crew by riding waves more easily, making little or no headway but considerable leeway. Boats vary in their ability to heave to, if properly balanced, a yacht will hold its position at about 60 to 70 degrees off the wind and will leave a slick of calm water to windward.

The method is to tack but keep the headsail backed. Hold or fasten the helm to leeward. Some modern designs are difficult to heave to since their efficient rigs continue to drive them forward. However, yachts can heave to under storm sails and have a steadier motion.

Going to windward (powered craft)

Motor cruisers can drive straight into head seas but it will be very uncomfortable for those on board, a better way uses a similar approach as sailing yachts. Rather than heading directly into the waves, dog-leg or tack across the waves, look for gaps between the breaking crests to head into and over the wave. If possible, trim the bow down. Use the throttle continuously and carefully to prevent the boat from flying off the wave or from digging into the trough.

Going downwind (sail craft)

Running before the wind will dramatically reduce the apparent wind speed and greatly reduce slamming.

However, the mainsail boom may dig into the water and slew the yacht around, so using a trysail and a storm jib—or either on their own—may be a better option.

Going downwind (powered craft)

Trim the bow up and position the boat on the back of a wave. After the wave breaks, drive through and on to the back of the next wave.

Big waves travel quickly, so keep a good lookout behind for waves catching you up.
Keep a hand on the throttle and control the boat speed carefully. You may need to slow down to prevent breaking through the wave and then speed up to get on the back of the next wave.

Drogues at sea

Drogues can be used on power or sail craft. They are attached to the stern of the boat and help prevent the yacht from being slewed sideways and rolled over by breaking waves in a following sea.

Use enough length of line—100 yards or 10 x the boat's length—to stop the drogue from breaking free of the water and at least two to three times the wave length. Because of the danger of being pooped by waves breaking over the stern, ensure that hatches, lockers and the companionway are secured.

If a drogue is not available, a length of heavy warp either in a line or a loop can be used.

Spread the load over several cleats and pad areas that are likely to chafe.

Drogues help prevent broaching and twisting sideways onto the waves.

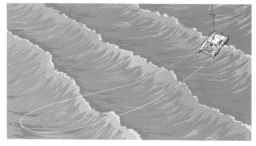

A long loop of trailing warp can also be used in a following sea.

Sea anchors

Deployed from the bow, and similar in size and shape to a parachute, a sea anchor keeps the bow head-to-wind and waves and reduces the possibility of capsize or pitch-poling. Sea anchors can be used on all types of craft but are particularly useful for catamarans and motor cruisers, which would otherwise turn their sterns towards the waves.

A sea anchor for a 30-foot yacht would be about 12 feet in diameter. As with a ground anchor, nylon warp or chain and warp will reduce snatching. A sea anchor should be deployed with sufficient length of warp to ensure it stays submerged, usually about two to three wave lengths, which may require about 100 yards of warp.

As with drogues and when using the normal anchor, spread the load over several strongpoints and pad it in areas likely to chafe.

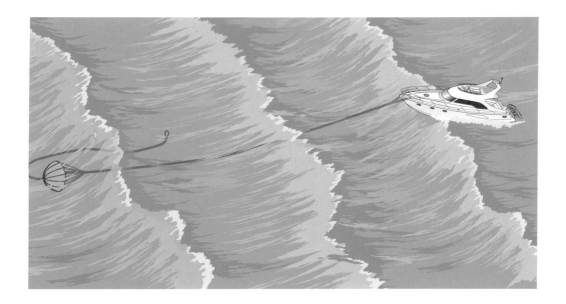

Damage control and repair

Your boat is your best liferaft. Unless it is about to sink, or is on fire, stay with it. It provides the best shelter, a large target for rescuers to see, and contains more provisions and equipment than a liferaft. Be prepared and improvise to keep your boat afloat.

The 1979 Fastnet Race

Winds reached Force 11 during the 1979 Fastnet Race. Over 300 yachts started the 605-mile race to the Fastnet Rock and back. Confused seas added to the ferocious conditions. Of the twenty-four yachts abandoned only five sank. Sadly, fifteen people lost their lives, seven after abandoning to their liferafts.

Steering failure

In heavy seas damage can be sustained to the steering system up to and including complete loss of the rudder, so all boats should carry an emergency steering system. If there is damage to the steering system, try to attach a temporary emergency tiller to the top of the rudder stock, or jury-rig a rope and blocks to the rudder quadrant.

Twin-engine boats can steer by using the engines separately. Auxiliary outboard powered boats can use the engine to steer and if fitted, a bow thruster may be able to point the boat in the right direction.

If the rudder is lost

A pre-drilled locker cover or washboard can be fastened to a spinnaker or whisper pole using U-bolts or lashings to create a steering oar or sweep. Use guys from winches to assist in steering and to stop the rudder floating.

Help in steering may be possible by dragging a drogue or bucket on a bridle to one side or other over the stern.

Jury rig a steering oar using the spinnaker pole and washboard or cabin locker cover.

Broken mast

Try to prevent mast breakage by keeping a close eye on standing rigging. The windward rigging is under tension and more likely to break—watch out for parting strands and try tacking to reduce tension on the shroud. Use a halyard to reinforce the shroud. A spinnaker pole may give a better lead. Watch out for leeward shroud turnbuckles that may have vibrated loose before tacking.

If the mast comes down

Clear away any broken spars quickly since they may hole the boat. Use cable cutters and a hacksaw (before going out ensure you have plenty of blades), a cartridge cutter or hydraulic cutter will cut rod rigging or rigging wire of over 10mm diameter. Try to keep the spars for jury-rigging a temporary mast and sail. The motion of the boat will change and the boat will become more susceptible to breaking waves. Advise approaching rescuers if any lines or spars are still in the water.

Jury rig

Use lateral thinking to jury-rig a temporary mast. Bulldog grips can be used to shorten and secure rigging wire and mainsheets, handybillys and vangs used to hoist or tension spars. Recut the sails if necessary.

Emergency VHF antenna

When the mast breaks it is likely the radio antenna will be damaged. Always carry an emergency VHF antenna to ensure communications.

Hatch damage

To seal a broken hatch use locker lids tourniqueted into position with a boat hook or deck brush. Better still, have pre-drilled hatch and portlight covers ready for emergency use.

Hull damage

A relatively small hole can let in a large amount of water in a very short time. The amount of water will depend on the size of hole and its depth below the waterline. For example, a 3in diameter hole about 1ft below the waterline will let in about half a ton of water in a minute, too much for bilge pumps to cope with.

Reducing the area of the hole even by partially blocking it will significantly reduce the flow rate. Block the hole with any materials you have available, braced against the opposite side of boat.

An alternative method is to cover the hole from outside using a sail or other waterproof fabric cover. Whether this is possible will depend on the position of the hole, the shape of the hull and the weather conditions.

Make sure the bilge pumps are able to reach all parts of the hull. Electric pumps will only continue to pump so long as they have electricity. Engine-driven pumps can shift considerable amounts of water. Ensure manual pumps are operational. All pumps should be fitted with strum boxes (filters) to prevent blockage.

Attach an appropriate-sized softwood bung to each seacock. If the skin fitting or hose breaks and a seacock has seized, the bung can be used to stem the flow.

CHAPTER 5 : Lifejackets and buoyancy aids

There are a broad range of lifejackets available on the market from stiff buoyant foam models suitable for merchant shipping, to the inflatable bladder types that you will see demonstrated on commercial airlines. Here we have restricted our comments to those commonly available to the boat user. An International ISO standard has recently taken effect and will supercede national standards as new designs are introduced.

Buoyancy Aids

Buoyancy aids are not recommended as life-saving equipment.

- **ISO 12402-5 buoyancy aids** are designed for competent swimmers as an aid to flotation in inshore waters where help is close at hand. They are suitable for those who expect to fall into the water, for example dinghy sailors, waterskiers, kayakers, etc.—allowing them to swim easily back to their craft. This type is comfortable to wear but will not turn the wearer face-up in the water. It provides 11lb (5 kg) of buoyancy from, usually, one or several layers of closed-cell foam.

Sold in several sizes from child to XXL, buoyancy aids need to be a snug fit to work properly. A simple test is to try lifting the jacket at the shoulders. If it lifts more than 2 inches (50mm) it's too big.

Lifejackets

- **ISO 12402-4 lifejackets** are designed to keep non-swimmers afloat but will not necessarily turn an unconscious wearer face-up. Usually made from one or several layers of closed-cell foam and provides 22lb or 10kg of buoyancy. Like buoyancy aids, they are sold in several sizes from child to XXL and need to be a tight fit to work properly. Check for fit by lifting the jacket at shoulders. If it lifts more than 2 inches (50mm) it's too big.

- **ISO 12402-3 lifejacket** is the standard lifejacket, providing a minimum buoyancy of 33lb (15kg). Suitable for swimmers and non-swimmers and is arguably the best type for offshore boats. Although this type is designed to turn an unconscious wearer face-up, if there is any air trapped in the wearer's waterproof clothing this may prevent the jacket from righting the person immediately.

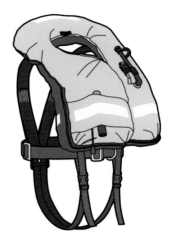

The lifejacket will give a reasonable chance of survival but will hamper movement when fully deployed. Most jackets of this size are gas-inflated; however, bulky all-foam or foam-and-air jackets are also available.

- **ISO 12402-2 lifejacket** was originally intended to provide sufficient buoyancy to self right an offshore oil worker wearing an immersion suit and is a high-performance lifejacket, suitable for severe offshore conditions. Usually gas-inflated and consisting of one or, occasionally, two separate bladders, it has sufficient buoyancy —60.5lb (27.5kg)—to counteract trapped air in waterproof clothing. Sadly, its large deployed size can make it difficult for the wearer to climb into a liferaft.

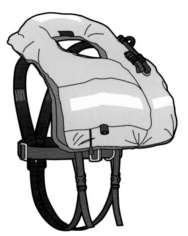

Children's lifejackets have equivalent buoyancy ratings to adults' lifejackets, for example, 50N and 150N, but with reduced buoyancy to suit their smaller size. Most have harnesses and crotch straps built in as standard. It's essential that children wear the correct size lifejacket or buoyancy aid. Don't buy a lifejacket that is too big thinking they will grow into it.

Top five lifejacket tips
- Carry one lifejacket for each member of the crew
- Carry spare lifejackets for any casualties you may pick up
- Always check your lifejacket before donning
- Lifejackets require regular maintenance
- Your lifejacket will only work properly if it is worn correctly

Gas lifejackets

Gas lifejackets are inflated with carbon dioxide (CO_2) stored under pressure in a sealed metal bottle. The gas is released by piercing the seal, either manually by pulling the toggle or automatically on immersion in water.

If fitted with an automatic firing head, it is essential to fit the correct size bottle for the size of lifejacket. Too big a bottle may burst the jacket; too small a bottle will not fully inflate the bladder. The correct size bottle will fully inflate the jacket in under five seconds.

- A lifejacket has to be worn outside of clothing. If it inflates underneath a waterproof jacket, the wearer's chest will be squeezed making it impossible to draw breath.
- Make sure that the manual-inflation toggle is always available—do not tuck it inside the jacket.

Types of inflation

Oral-only inflation (blow air into)
Inflatable lifejackets that can only be inflated through a top-up tube are not recommended. Due to the physiological effects of falling into cold water, you will not be able to inflate the lifejacket.

Manual gas inflation
It will not inflate automatically, the jacket is inflated by the wearer pulling on the toggle. The firing mechanism should have some means of indicating if the jacket has been fired—often it is as simple as a small green clip over the toggle lever. If this is not present, unscrew and check that the seal on the bottle has not been pierced—if in doubt, rearm.

Always carry spare gas bottles and clips so that the lifejacket can be immediately rearmed.

Pull
↓

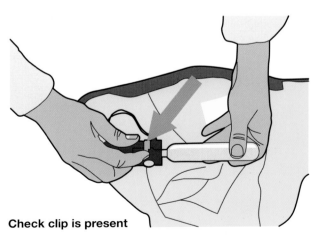

Check clip is present

Automatic gas/cartridge inflation

There are several different designs of automatic gas-inflation firing heads that give various degrees of protection to the cartridge or pill. Automatic operation uses a spring-loaded plunger held in place by either a compacted paper cartridge or a pill. When the cartridge or pill becomes wet it expands or dissolves, releasing the plunger so that it pushes the pin through the gas-bottle seal.

In addition to a manual indicator, automatic firing mechanisms have a separate indicator to show they have not been operated. When donning the lifejacket, check the automatic firing head and the manual indicators. If one or other is not present, unscrew and check that the seal on the bottle has not been pierced.

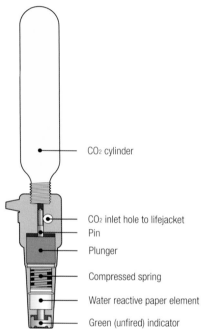

CO_2 cylinder

CO_2 inlet hole to lifejacket
Pin
Plunger

Compressed spring

Water reactive paper element

Green (unfired) indicator

While some lifejackets use cartridge style autoheads others have a simple replaceable bobbin. Although different makes of lifejackets may appear to have identical firing heads they are often not interchangeable. Some automatic firing heads can fire accidentally if they become excessively wet. Keep appropriate spare automatic firing heads and gas bottles on board so that every lifejacket can be immediately rearmed.

Green (unfired) indicator

Standard automatic heads have a limited life and will be marked with an expiration date.

Red (fired) indicator

Hammar automatic inflation

The Hammar system protects the water-sensitive element with a hydrostatic valve that prevents accidental activation by wave splash, heavy rain or spray. The valve opens after two to three seconds' immersion at a depth of 4 inches. This allows water to reach the water-sensitive element, which dissolves and triggers the pin to pierce the bottle.

When the jacket is fired manually, the toggle detaches from the firing head. The firing head will show a green indicator if it has not been fired or a red one if it has. Hammar automatic inflation heads have a five-year life. The replacement date is printed on the firing head. Keep spare rearming kits on board so that the jacket can be rearmed immediately and check they have not passed their expiration date. Inflate the lifejacket after rearming, to check the head has sealed properly on to the fabric.

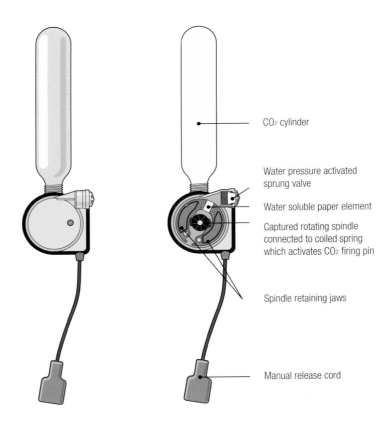

CO_2 cylinder

Water pressure activated sprung valve

Water soluble paper element

Captured rotating spindle connected to coiled spring which activates CO_2 firing pin

Spindle retaining jaws

Manual release cord

Lifejacket maintenance and checks

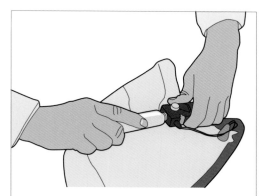

Regularly check that the gas bottle is securely tightened into the firing mechanism. If it is loose, it may not fire and inflate the jacket.

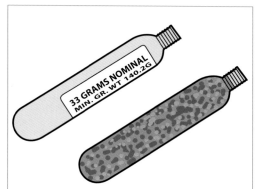

Inspect the gas bottle for corrosion, which can cause small pinholes in the lifejacket bladder. Check that the bottle is the correct capacity for the lifejacket.

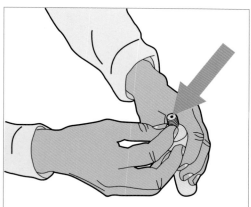

Unscrew the bottle and check the seal is still secure. If it has a hole in it, fit a replacement bottle.

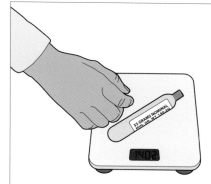

Weigh the bottle on a digital scale to ensure it matches its gross weight as embossed on the bottle. A 33g bottle has a gross weight around 140g.

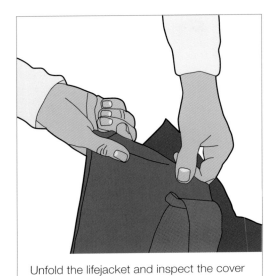

Unfold the lifejacket and inspect the cover and bladder for punctures, cracks and wear and tear.

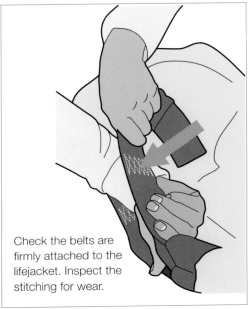

Check the belts are firmly attached to the lifejacket. Inspect the stitching for wear.

To deflate, push in the valve in the oral inflation tube while squeezing the jacket. Make sure all gas is removed before reattaching a new gas cylinder and repacking.

Every three to six months

- Remove the gas bottle and inflate the jacket, preferably with an air pump, through the oral inflation tube.
- Leave the jacket inflated for 24 hours to check that it is airtight.
- When not being used regularly, unfold the jacket and store it on a wooden clothes hanger.

> **Tip**
> Not all manufacturers air-test their lifejackets at every appropriate stage in its manufacture, so it's a good practice immediately after purchase to inflate all new jackets, preferably using an air pump through the oral tube, to ensure the bladder does not leak.

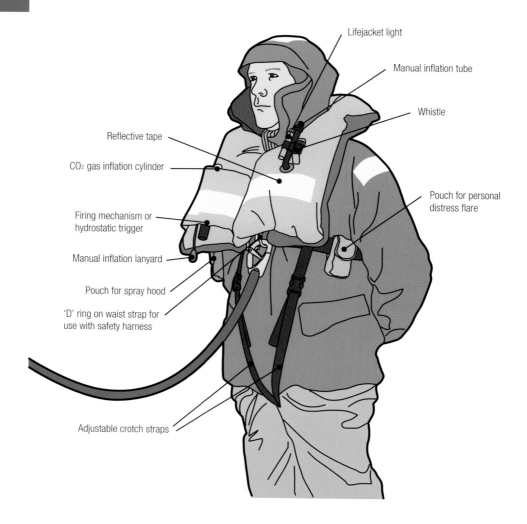

Lifejacket light

Manual inflation tube

Whistle

Reflective tape

CO₂ gas inflation cylinder

Pouch for personal distress flare

Firing mechanism or hydrostatic trigger

Manual inflation lanyard

Pouch for spray hood

'D' ring on waist strap for use with safety harness

Adjustable crotch straps

Lifejacket fittings

Some jackets are sold with a number of fittings as standard, for example, the whistle, oral inflation tube, retro-reflective tape and gas inflation system. But other fittings such as the crotch straps, lifejacket light, built-in safety harness, safety harness, spray hood, and flare pouch, are often optional extras. It is recommended to always use a lifejacket fitted with a light, spray hood, and crotch straps.

The effect of wind and waves

When at rest in the water, the wearer of a lifejacket will be continuously turned to face the wind and waves. While a conscious casualty can cover their airway, an unconscious one will drown from waves and spray continually breaking onto their face.

A spray hood, either fitted into the collar of the lifejacket or stored in a separate pouch on the waist belt, can be worn over the head or face and will reduce the effects of breaking waves.

Donning a gas-inflated lifejacket

You should be able to put on and fasten your lifejacket in less than 30 seconds, so practice until you can.

It's essential the lifejacket is worn correctly. If it is too slack the wearer may slip down or even out of the jacket while in the water or being lifted aboard a boat. The lifejacket needs to keep the airway as high above the water as possible. Crotch or thigh straps hold the lifejacket down and lift the body up and, therefore, the airway higher above the water. Wear your lifejacket at all times when on deck. Once it is adjusted to fit you, keep your lifejacket close to hand when below decks, so that it can be donned quickly.

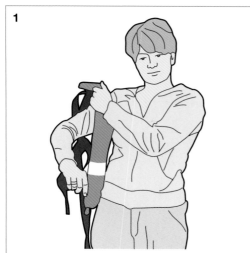

1

Put the jacket on like a waistcoat. Hold the jacket the right way up and put your right arm between the jacket front and the back strap.

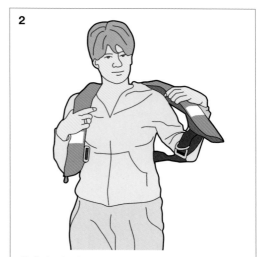

2

Pull the jacket across your back and put your left arm between left jacket front and the back strap.

Buddy check

It's good practice to ask another crew member to check you are wearing the lifejacket correctly.

3

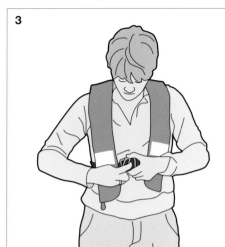

Straighten the waist belt and fasten the clip at the front of the jacket. Check it is secure.

4

Reach down and pull the crotch strap or thigh straps between your legs and clip it to the waist belt. Shorten the straps to take up the slack but not so tightly as to be uncomfortable.

5

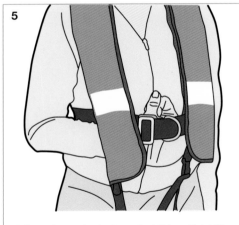

Adjust the waist belt so that it is a tight fit when your fist is placed between the strap and your chest. This will prevent the jacket from squeezing your chest when it inflates and without making it too slack.

Tip

- Stow lifejackets where they can be reached quickly

- Each crew member to have their own lifejacket already adjusted to size

- Add a colored tag to make the lifejacket easier to identify

- Write your name and the boat's name on the back of the service label in indelible ink

- Don't think when to put your lifejacket on, consider when to take it off!

CHAPTER 6 : MOB prevention

Staying on board your boat is preferable to falling overboard! Clip on. Do not go on deck unnecessarily in heavy conditions and clip on if you must. When moving around remember the rule—one hand for the boat, one for yourself. Prevent accidents by clearing away unnecessary clutter and other hazards. Wear non-slip shoes or boots and avoid standing on ropes or sails since these can roll or slide underfoot. Try to avoid stepping on to smooth wet surfaces such as shiny fiberglass. Wash off oil or diesel spills especially from sidedecks.

Regularly check lifelines and stanchions are firmly attached. Lifelines should be ready to be released or cut easily to aid MOB recovery. A "Granny bar" at the mast of a sailing yacht helps to steady crew when working at the mast.

Ensure the helmsman warns the crew of maneuvers—avoid sudden acceleration or surprise tacks or gybes. Look out and warn other crew of larger-than-normal approaching waves.

Clipping on

There are many factors which determine the need to clip on. On displacement sailing yachts, wear a safety harness or, preferably, a lifejacket with a built-in safety harness and "clip on." Strong attachment eyes should be fitted in the cockpit just outside the companionway so that crew can clip on before leaving the cabin. Other eyes can be fitted in the cockpit so that the crew can move away from the companionway.

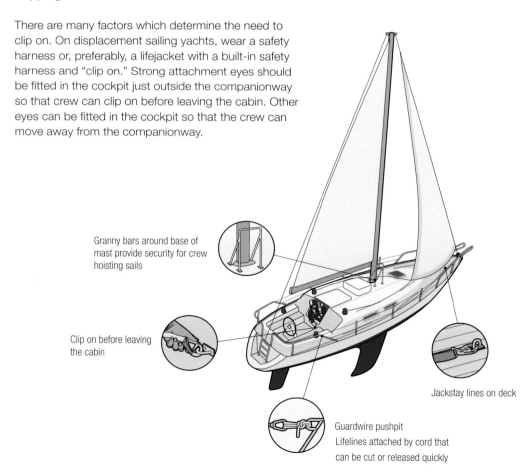

Granny bars around base of mast provide security for crew hoisting sails

Clip on before leaving the cabin

Jackstay lines on deck

Guardwire pushpit
Lifelines attached by cord that can be cut or released quickly

In heavy weather, only go on deck if necessary and clip on to a jackstay. Keep your center of gravity low—crawl if necessary. Tell the helmsman or skipper before going on deck. On sailing boats go forward on the windward side.

Use a harness with locking snap hooks, such as Gibb Hooks or Wichard Hooks. A three-hook safety harness allows crew to clip onto the next strongpoint before unclipping. Safety lines should have a safety hook at all ends so that the crew can unclip themselves quickly. Jackstays may be made from polyester webbing or stainless-steel wire, webbing jackstays are degraded by sunlight so check and replace them regularly. Wire jackstays can roll underfoot.

Fast boats

It is advisable not to clip-on to planing or semi-displacement boats. It is better to fall clear since being dragged alongside a hull at high speed will cause severe injury.

Never clip onto a motorboat when it is moving at speed.

However, if the boat has stopped or is moving at under 5 knots, you can clip on when going on deck, for example, when going forward to drop anchor in heavy weather. Motorboats seldom have jackstays fitted but there is no reason why they cannot be fitted.

CHAPTER 7 : MOB

MOB actions to be taken by crew

1. Shout "man overboard" to alert the crew.
2. Press the MOB button on the GPS.
3. Throw a life-buoy and dan buoy to the MOB. Mark the MOB with a buoyant smoke flare.
4. Allocate a crew member to point at the MOB in the water.
5. Send a DSC distress alert and a voice Mayday.
6. Keep pointing. Don't lose sight of the MOB.
7. On a sailing boat, the skipper will ask for the jib to be lowered or furled and the engine started.
8. Prepare a throwing line.
9. The skipper will bring the boat alongside the MOB, with the boat pointing into wind and the propeller stopped.
10. Get a line around the MOB and get them aboard.

MOB search patterns

These search patterns are for a boat to follow when looking for a man overboard who has been lost from sight. Press the MOB button on the GPS receiver as soon as possible after the person falls overboard. This will record a geographical position and a bearing and distance to that point.

Press the DSC distress alert, choose "MOB" from the menu options and send a voice Mayday. If short -handed, there may not be time to send a voice Mayday immediately. The MOB is unlikely to be at the recorded position but it will provide a datum for calculating where they will drift due to wind and current.

Sector search

A good datum is required. Sector search is good for searching small areas. Mark the datum point with a dan buoy, a life buoy with drogue, a weighted fender or similar. The marker should be able to drift with the tide but not be blown by the wind.

Go North (000 degree) first (some prefer to go downdrift first but this can make the sums more complicated). When moving away from the marker, count out loud glancing at the marker. When the marker is visible for only 50% of the time, that is the distance that indicates the Expected Detection Range (EDR). Measure each leg by counting aloud. It is suggested that each leg is three times the EDR. At the end of each leg, turn 120 degrees to starboard and proceed for the same distance.

If the search is not successful after the first circuit, reorientate the search by 30 degrees to starboard.

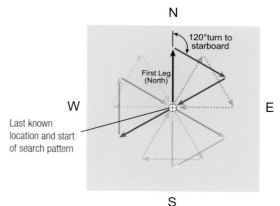

All turns are 120° to starboard. On completion of first search pattern (colored) rotate by 30° as shown by dotted line

Sector Search

Expanding box search

If the datum point is a little unreliable or a sector search has not proved successful, an expanding box search should be started.

Usually, the leg length is 75% of the EDR. If a sector search has been completed, this will be the third search of the area, in which case it is acceptable to use a leg length of 100% EDR.

For ease of use, it is suggested that the headings are North, East, South and West. Count aloud to measure the distance.

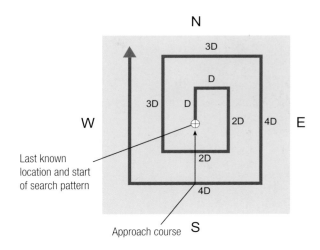

Expanding Box Search

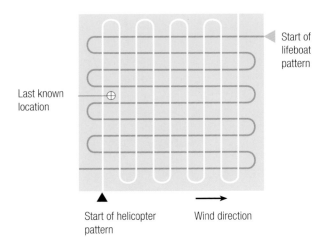

SAR Search Pattern

SAR search pattern

To search large areas where the position of the casualty is unknown, the Coast Guard will task the SAR units to undertake a parallel search pattern. If lifeboat and helicopter are both involved, their tracks are likely to be at 90 degrees to each other to increase the chances of detection.

Sailing yacht MOB maneuver

It will be quicker and safer to use the engine to return to the MOB. But if it won't start or the propeller is fouled, use the sails. Make sure the crew are practiced in MOB recovery procedures.

Under sail

1. Sheet in the mainsail and heave to to slow the boat. Pass buoyancy to the casualty and mark with a dan buoy. Instruct a crew member to point at the MOB. Retrieve any warps in the water and start the engine.
2. If the engine is not working turn onto beam/broad reach and sail away.
3. Sail about five to six boat-lengths from the MOB. Do not lose sight of MOB.
4. Tack. Aim the leeward side of yacht at the MOB or the marker. Let out the headsail and mainsail sheets. The mainsail should flap; if not, bear off downwind to change the angle of approach. Point the boat back at the MOB until the mainsail flaps.
5. The angle of approach should be a close reach so that the sails can be powered and depowered. Drop the headsail if there is sufficient power from the mainsail alone.
6. Fill and spill the mainsail and slowly approach the MOB. Pick up the MOB to leeward, aft of the mast.

Under power

1. Sheet in the mainsail and heave to to slow the boat. Pass buoyancy to the casualty and mark with a dan buoy. Instruct a crew member to point at the MOB. Retrieve any warps in the water and start the engine.
2. Furl or drop the headsail.
3. Make ready the throwing line.
4. Maneuver the boat downwind of the MOB, keeping the MOB in sight.
5. Approach the MOB into the wind so that the mainsail is depowered. Pick up the MOB on the leeward side, aft of the mast.

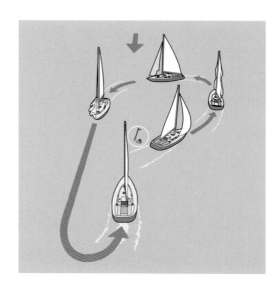

Powerboat MOB maneuver

The Williamson Turn is designed to turn the motorboat onto a reciprocal track.

1. Note the compass heading and add 60 degrees.
2. Turn to starboard on to the new course; note the amount of helm used.
3. When you reach the heading, turn the helm in the opposite direction at the same rate as before.
4. As you reach the reciprocal heading or you see your original track in the water, straighten the wheel.
5. Slow down and look for the MOB.

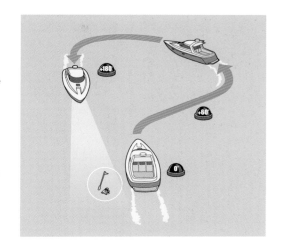

Approaching the MOB

In rough weather, it will be best to approach from downwind, keeping the bow into the wind, taking care not to run over the MOB.

1. Pick the MOB up on the leeward side.
2. Stop engines when the MOB is alongside.
3. Use a throw line if unable to get close to a conscious MOB and pull them to the boat.

> **Note**
>
> If the helm position is on the starboard side, try to leave the MOB to starboard so that they can be seen more easily.

In acceptable conditions, position the boat across the wind, upwind of the MOB.

1. Keep the boat sideways-on to the wind and allow it to blow the boat towards the MOB.
2. Pick the MOB up on leeward side.
3. Stop the engines when the MOB is alongside.

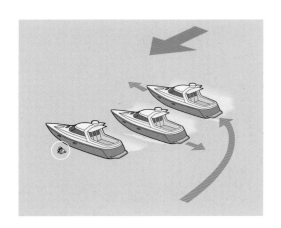

MOB recovery methods

Lifting a person out of the water requires planning and practice. It is a difficult task, especially for short-handed crews.

It's essential to get the person out of the water as quickly as possible. In very calm conditions it may be possible to retrieve them using the bathing platform or the ladder at the transom. However, in rougher seas this will be a dangerous place to attempt to recover a MOB, as the casualty is likely to be drawn under the stern of the boat and injured.

How you go about the task will depend on how your boat is set up and how long the person has been in the water. Hypothermic casualties should be recovered in a horizontal position and handled with care.

It may be easiest and quickest to launch the liferaft, and for a crew member to enter the raft dry and pull the MOB into the raft. This method is not without risk and the raft will not be available should you need it later in the voyage. Lower either the lowest or both guardrail wires along the side of the boat to ease recovery.

Crew dealing with MOB recovery should ensure that they are attached to the boat with a safety line. One MOB is enough.

Recovery methods for sailing yachts

Parbuckle
The Parbuckle is set on the side of the boat. The foot is fastened along the gunwale and the head attached either to a handybilly (block and tackle) that is attached to a halyard or to the halyard alone.

Lower the Parbuckle into the water and position the MOB.

Heave in on the handybilly—use a sheet winch for greater mechanical advantage.

The casualty will roll inside the parbuckle up and on to the sidedeck.

A small headsail can be used in place of a purpose-designed parbuckle. However, it will be more difficult to get the sail to sink sufficiently to position the MOB in it. Also there's a strong possibility that the MOB will slip out of the sail as they are being brought aboard.

MOB recovery raft

Proprietary MOB recovery rafts can also be lifted on board using a handybilly attached to the halyard or the boom lift.

Fastening to the top of the raft is easier than attaching to a MOB in the water. The rafts are easy to get into and minimize hydrostatic squeeze.

Boom lift

On yachts with booms not fitted with solid kickers, it may be possible to use the boom as a derrick. The yacht needs to be sufficiently large to withstand lifting a MOB on the boom.

The main sheet, attached with snap shackles at both ends, is reversed and freed from the deck fitting.

Slacken off the kicker and scandalise the boom to an angle of about 30 degrees from the horizontal. It may be necessary to back up the topping lift with the halyard.

Attach the bottom of the sheet either to the MOB's lifejacket or harness or to a rescue strop. Place the rescue strop around the MOB's chest.

Heave on the mainsheet or redirect the free end to a sheet winch and lift the MOB into the yacht.

A horizontal lift can be achieved by placing an additional safety lanyard or line behind the knees of the MOB.

Elevator method

Developed in the United States, the elevator method provides a quick way of helping a conscious MOB out of the water.

A line is attached to a forward cleat and led aft outside of the guard wires, fed through the headsail fairlead to the sheet winch. The MOB stands on the line as it is winched tight, thereby lifting the MOB up the side of the boat. In most cases a second line will need to be rigged over the side of the boat for the MOB to hold on to.

> Some motorboats may be able to adapt this method by rigging the line from a stern cleat, through the bow roller and on to the windlass.

Recovery method for motorboats

MOB recovery on a motorboat is more difficult than on sailing yachts due to the lack of rigging.

Many motor cruisers carry a small inflatable dinghy in davits or on snap davits attached to the transom bathing ladder. A quick method of MOB recovery is to lower the dinghy and recover the MOB into the dinghy. Make sure helping crew are attached to the boat.

If the MOB is too heavy to lift into the dinghy, one of the sponsons can be deflated and the MOB rolled into the dinghy.

CHAPTER 8 : Liferafts

Liferafts are designed should your boat sink or catch fire to get you out of the water and provide shelter for a limited period. Whenever possible, let the SAR services know you are abandoning to a liferaft so that they know what they are looking for.

The quality of liferafts varies enormously. Some products marked as a liferaft may be no more than a couple of gas-inflated floats: others provide an acceptable, stable, sheltered environment. Always look inside the canister if buying a secondhand raft—it has been known for unscrupulous sellers to replace the raft with bricks!

Basic leisure rafts

Usually at the lower end of the price scale, leisure liferafts are not made to any national or International standard or specification. Nor are they approved for any commercial operation, yachts sailing under racing rules or Class XII craft. The leisure liferaft is light in weight (easier for launching), and may or may not have a canopy. Some may have only one buoyancy chamber and minimal survival equipment as standard, but this is better than nothing in an emergency situation.

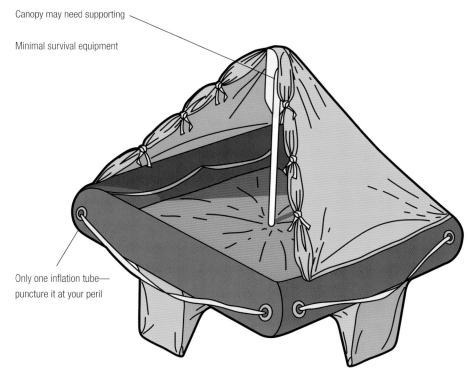

Canopy may need supporting

Minimal survival equipment

Only one inflation tube—
puncture it at your peril

Basic Leisure Liferaft

Inflatable Active Survival Craft

A number of offshore racing associations approve some makes of active survival craft as an alternative for a liferaft. However, most national authorities do not accept them as suitable safety equipment because there is currently no recognized standard for active survival craft.

Many are based on an inflatable dinghy fitted with a liferaft gas inflation system and a canopy for shelter. While the craft can be rowed or sailed to safety, the lack of ballast pockets make them unstable in a seaway.

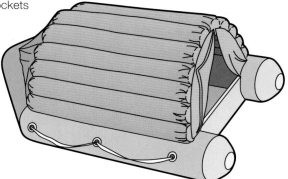

Since some areas have minimal rescue services, many bluewater sailors design their own survival craft, based on an inflatable or rigid dinghy with a small rig that allows them to effect their own rescue. However, these may not always be able to be readied and launched as quickly as a liferaft.

Liferaft standards

SOLAS

Commercial vessels have been required to carry liferafts built to SOLAS Standards, as detailed in Chapter IV of the Life Saving Appliances (LSA) code, since 1959. This standard has been periodically upgraded and SOLAS rafts are made and tested to high standards and extremes of operating temperatures. They are approximately 30% heavier, tougher and significantly more expensive than ISAF or ISO rafts. The Standard covers rafts from six-person capacity upwards.

ORC

The Offshore Racing Congress specification was introduced after the 1979 Fastnet Race inquiry. Yachts racing under their rules were required to carry ORC rafts. This has now been superseded by the ISAF Part II specification up until June 2007. ORC rafts built before December 2002 could still be fitted to ISAF racing yachts. However, this is no longer allowed. ORC rafts may still be found on many cruising yachts. ORC is also known as ISAF Part I and is in the ISAF Offshore Special Regulations.

ISAF

Following the 1998 Sydney–Hobart Race, the International Sailing Federation, (which now oversees the majority of offshore sail yacht racing in place of the ORC), developed a specification for liferafts similar to the ISO standard, principally as an interim measure while the new ISO standard was being completed. Although similar there are differences between ISAF and ISO. The ISAF specification came into force on 1st January 2003 and covers rafts of maximum capacities of 4 to 12 persons.

Note that ISAF specifies that Category 0 (zero) yachts should carry SOLAS rafts. The specification is included in Appendix A part 2 of ISAF's Offshore Special Regulations. (www.sailing.org)

ISO 9650 Small Craft—Inflatable Liferafts

Introduced by the International Standards Organization during 2005, ISO 9650 comprises of three parts:

Part 1:	Type 1 Liferafts for offshore use subdivided into: Group A rafts designed to inflate in temperatures of between –15 and +65°C. (5°F and 149°F) Group B rafts that will inflate between 0 and +65°C (air temperature). (32°F and 149°F)
Part 2:	Type 2 Liferafts for coastal use. All Part 2 rafts are expected to inflate between 0 and +65 degrees C.
Part 3:	Material to be used in liferaft manufacture

The main differences between Part 1: Type 1 and Part 2: Type 2 rafts are shown in the table. Type 2 rafts are, size for size, slightly smaller than Type 1 rafts. Type 1 rafts are more robust than Type 2 rafts. Type 1 Group A liferafts are recommended for northern European waters.

	ISO 9650 Part 1: Type 1	ISO 9650 Part 2: Type 2
Maximum Capacities	4 person to 12 person	4 person to 10 person
Painter length	9 meters	6 meters
Withstand drop of	6 meters	4 meters
Minimum Freeboard	4 person = 250mm 6 person+ = 300mm	4 person = 200mm 6 person+ = 250mm
Floor	Grp A rafts include thermal floor	Optional

Liferafts built to ISO 9650 Part 1: Type 1 are given a choice of two equipment packs depending on expected duration at sea—less than 24 hours and more than 24 hours (see Liferaft packs on p.62).

ORC, ISAF, ISO 9650 and SOLAS specify that the liferaft's main buoyancy is divided into two separate chambers. Each chamber must have sufficient buoyancy to support the maximum capacity of the raft. The chambers must be able to be topped up with a bellows and have pressure-relief valves. Each standard also specifies that the liferaft must have a canopy.

Which size raft?

The capacity of the liferaft(s) should be sufficient to carry all persons on board. However, if regularly sailing short-handed, it may be advisable to obtain two smaller rafts instead of one large raft. An added advantage being that the smaller rafts will be lighter and easier to handle. In addition to the ballast pockets, a liferaft uses the weight of its crew to keep it stable in waves. For example a boat that can carry eight people would have two four-person rafts instead of one eight-person raft if the boat was regularly sailed by a crew of only two or four.

Typical leisure raft

There are a number of mid-range yacht liferafts that do not meet ORC, ISAF, ISO or SOLAS standards. Their prices are lower but the quality of construction is also lower and there are often very few fittings included.

ISAF, ISO 9650 Part 1 and SOLAS

Externally there are few differences between liferafts built to SOLAS, ISO 9650 Part 1:Type 1 and ISAF. However, as a guide, SOLAS rafts are more robust than ISO/ISAF rafts, which in turn are more robust than non-standard rafts.

SOLAS rafts are designed to:

- withstand exposure for 30 days afloat (compared with 20 days for ISO/ISAF).
- withstand stowage in temperatures from -22°F to 140°F (–30 to +60 degrees C).
- withstand a drop from 20 yards (18 meters) and withstand persons jumping repeatedly into them from 5 yards (4.5 meters).

SOLAS rafts have lined canopies to provide insulation. Fig. 1 is a raft that includes the correct fittings to meet these standards.

Inflatable radar reflector

Drogue attached to the opposite side to the entrance

Reflective tape

Automatically activated light

Auto inflation canopy arch

Internal light

Resealable waterproof bag for loose contents

Printed instructions on inside of canopy

Lookout port

Internal grab lines

6 PERSONS

Closeable entrance door

Pocket for SART pole or radar reflector

Rain catchment system

High visibilty double lined orange canopy

External lifelines

Safety knife

Hand straps to help pull yourself in

Inflatable or thermoreflective floor

ENTER HERE

Inflatable ramp

Twin buoyancy compartments

Painter

Ballast bags for increased stability and reduced drift

CO_2 gas inflation cylinder

Entry ladder

Fig. 1

Canister v Valise

Liferafts are supplied in either a plastic/fiberglass box or in a fabric valise. To protect from water damage, most rafts—canister and valise—are vacuum-packed in large polythene bags that rip open when the raft inflates.

Canister
The canister is usually made from two parts held together with straps and provides a hard case to protect the raft from knocks and sharp objects. The canister is not waterproof but the packaging inside should prevent ingress of water.

Pros	*Cons*
• Usually easily accessible	• More likely to be stolen or washed overboard
• Contents protected from damage	• More expensive to buy
• Can be used with an HRU (see p.60)	• Prone to damage from the elements

Valise rafts
These need to be stowed in a dedicated weatherproof locker. A valise should never be left strapped to an exposed deck or buried deep in a locker under piles of sails, fenders, or warps. Make sure it is always readily available.

Pros	*Cons*
• Cheaper to buy	• Likely to be damaged by rough handling —do not throw them on to pontoons
• Easier to move because they have handles and are lighter in weight than a rigid canister	• Harder to deploy because they have to be lifted out of a locker
• Less likely to be washed overboard	• Cannot be automatically deployed
	• Cannot be left in an exposed position

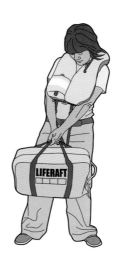

Liferaft stowage

A liferaft is a heavy and sometimes awkward
piece of kit to carry. Apart from the smallest
rafts, most will require a two-man lift. As you
are likely to need it in a hurry, you need to give
careful consideration as to where to stow it.

Ideally, the raft needs to be positioned so that it
is readily accessible yet is protected from heavy
weather.

Canister rafts can be deck-mounted on the
coachroof, in the cockpit, on the bathing
platform, on the transom, or in a purpose-made
bracket on the pushpit.

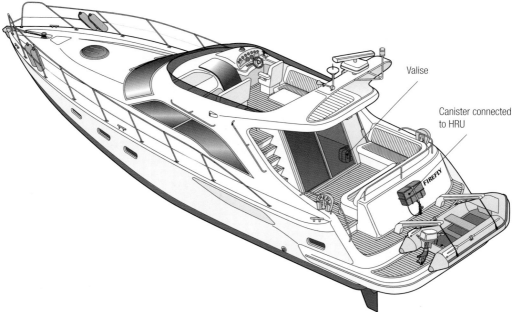

Valise

Canister connected
to HRU

If stowed vertically in a bracket the raft may need to be specially packed to prevent the weight of the cylinder damaging the raft material. The canister's drain holes may also need to be repositioned.

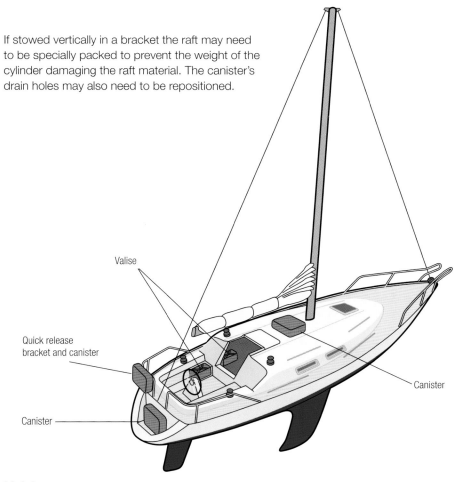

Valise

Quick release bracket and canister

Canister

Canister

Maintenance

Make sure that a competent service agent services your liferaft at the manufacturer's required periods. Most modern rafts are vacuum-packed in large plastic bags, and if stored correctly should extend the service period to three years. However, there are still many rafts that need to be serviced annually. Good service centers will let you view the liferaft inflated and check the quality and amount of equipment packed with the raft.

Renting

In most countries, it is possible to rent a liferaft from a liferaft rental center. Rafts can be rented for periods from as little as a week right through to a whole season or more. This may be particularly useful for those that sail short-handed with one raft for most of the year and only occasionally with a full crew, when two rafts are needed.

Hydrostatic release units (HRUs)

Boats can sink within minutes if their hull is breached by even a relatively small hole. Fast craft are especially susceptible to high-speed impacts and have been known to sink in under 30 seconds! Commercial craft are required to fit HRUs to their liferaft.

How an HRU works

The HRU automatically cuts the securing strap holding the raft in place when the boat sinks to a depth between 3 to 13 feet (1 and 4 meters). The painter remains attached to the HRU weak link and the raft has sufficient buoyancy to float to the surface.

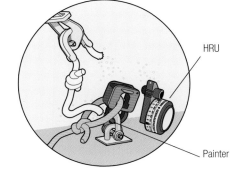

HRU

Painter

As the boat sinks further, it tugs on the painter to trigger the inflation system.

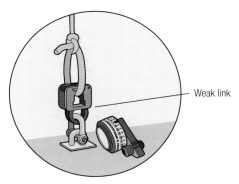

Weak link

The greater buoyancy of the inflated raft is sufficient to break the weak link and releases the painter from the boat.

If the boat sinks in shallow water it may be necessary to release the liferaft manually.

It's essential that the HRU is properly installed, because otherwise the raft will not break free and inflate. Illustrated below are new and old versions of the disposable Hammar HRU often used on boats. More expensive serviceable units are also available.

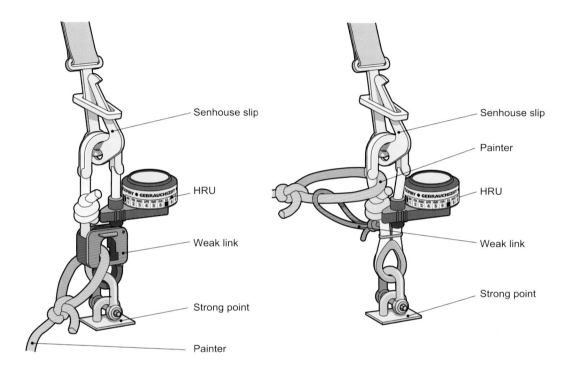

HRU safety checks

The Hammar HRU is a replaceable unit with a two-year lifespan. The expiration date should be marked on the unit. Replace it when required.

Check that no other straps (or padlocks) are used to secure the liferaft.

The ring on the Senhouse slip should be checked periodically to make sure it is free as vibration can cause the ring to jam in place, making it difficult to launch the raft manually.

Liferaft packs

Generally, the contents of a liferaft will depend on the type of raft: leisure, ORC, ISAF, ISO 9650, or SOLAS. Listed on page 63 are the minimum contents required under each specification. Note that ISO 9650 Part 1: Type 1 rafts have a choice of packs suitable for survival for under 24 hours or over 24 hours. You specify which pack when you purchase or service the liferaft.

The standard pack can be supplemented with extra equipment as long as it can fit in. Check contents with your service agent. If there is no room for the item you need, add it to your grab bag. Carefully consider what you may need for the area you will be sailing.

Find out what you have in your liferaft before you need it.

Many items inside the raft will have a limited life—flares, water, food, etc.—and need to be replaced when the raft is serviced. When possible, check the quality of equipment in your raft—cheap rafts may have poor-quality equipment—for example childrens' beach spades for paddles!.

Some raft packs pack equipment that you will need immediately in a separate pack.

Buoyant safety knife—attached with a lanyard and usually found in a sheath next to the raft entrance. Use it to safely cut the painter as close to the yacht as possible; keep the line, it may be useful later.

Bailer—it may be no more than a fabric dish, boots are much more effective but only as a last resort because you will suffer heat loss if they are removed. It's difficult to bail with the door closed, a stirrup pump is more effective, so pack one in your grab bag. The bailer can also be used as a sick bucket or a toilet—this is safer than leaning out of the doorway. Some liferafts may be fitted with an integral bailer, check manufacturer's usage instructions.

Sponges—the number supplied will depend on the raft pack. They usually come "flat-packed" and dry. Use one to help dry out the raft. The other should be kept uncontaminated and used to collect drinking water by wiping condensation from inside the raft canopy.

Paddles—are essential for moving clear of a burning yacht or other hazard and very useful for maneuvering to pick up survivors from the water. They are usually but not always in two parts and can also be used as a splint for broken limbs.

Whistle—this is more effective than shouting.

Item	Solas A	Solas B	Iso 9650 24 hours or more	Iso 9650 less than 24 hours	ISAF	ORC	Typical leisure raft (D-pack)
Buoyant knife	1	1	1	1	1	1	1
Bailer	1	1	1	1	1	1	1
Sponges	2	2	2	2	1pp	2	2
Paddles	2	2	2	2	2	2	2
Whistle	1	1	1	1	1	1	-
Torches	1	1	1	1	2	1	-
Heliograph	1	1	1	1	1	-	-
Anti seasick pills	6pp	6pp	6pp	6pp	6pp	-	-
Seasick bag	1pp	1pp	1pp	1pp	1pp	-	-
Red h/h flares	6	3	6	3	3	3	-
Para rocket flares	4	2	2	2	Grab bag	-	-
Buoyant smoke flare	2	1	-	-	-	-	-
TPA	2	2	2	-	2	-	-
Repair kit	1	1	1	1	1	1	1
Water	1 pt pp	-	1pt pp	-	Grab bag	-	-
Food	2,400 cal pp		2,400 cal pp	-	Grab bag	-	-
First Aid kit	1	1	1	-	1	-	-
Bellows	1	1	1	1	1	1	1
Throwing line – 30m	1	1	1	1	1		1
Drogue	2	2	1	1	2	1	1
Waterproof notebook	-	-	-	-	1	-	-
Signal card	1	1	-	-	-	1	1
Sea Survival instructions	-	-	-	-	1	-	1
Leak stoppers	Set	Set	-	-	Set	Set	-
Radar reflector	1	1	-	-	-	-	-
Fishing kit	1	-	-	-	-	-	-
Tin opener	3	-	-	-	-	-	-
Graduated drinking cup	1	-	-	-	-	-	-

pp = per person

Torches—these usually come packed with only one set of spare batteries and bulb or there may be two sealed torches so make sure you pack sufficient spares. They are essential for looking for other casualties and for signalling in the dark.

Heliograph (signaling mirror)—easy to use and effective for daytime signalling. If no sight is provided, use your fingers. Hold out your arm and put up two fingers between you and the target. Direct the sunlight on to your fingers. You can use a CD to practice with, but be aware that water may dissolve the shiny surface, so they are not a suitable long-term alternative.

Anti-seasickness pills—should be taken as soon as possible, preferably before entering the raft.

Seasickness bag—only one per person is supplied in rafts made to the Standards, using them keeps the interior a little more habitable.

Flares—are arguably the most important pieces of equipment on the liferaft. The number and type will depend on the type of pack. Make sure you and your crew are familiar with the triggering methods and use of the different types because what are supplied in the raft may be different to those on your boat. Keep them dry and do not use them until you are confident they will be seen.

TPA (thermal protective aid)—not found on all rafts. Used to reduce heat loss of wet casualties, use by wringing out their clothes and redressing the casualty, then place the casualty in the TPA. Some TPAs are big enough for two people at one time.

Repair kit—the standard repair kit consists of patches and glue not dissimilar to those used to repair bicycle inner tubes, needs to be used in dry conditions. Many rafts are now also supplied with liferaft repair clamps and/or leak-stopper bungs that can seal holes quickly in wet or dry conditions.

Water—if included, will be only half a liter per person. Supplement this with extra rations or keep a desalinator in the grab bag.

Food—the type varies but it will be carbohydrate-based and should provide 2,400 calories per person.

First-aid kit—the contents will vary with the quality of the raft. The SOLAS C kit provides a comprehensive selection of equipment. Supplement your grab bag with extra medical supplies or any specific medications you need.

Bellows—used to top up the sponsons and for inflating the inflatable floor. Take care not to suck up water. Tie the bellows in because if you lose it you will need to top up the tubes by mouth. If possible take an extra pump from boat.

Throwing line and quoit—usually 33 yards (30 meters) long. If you are unable to paddle to other casualties, throw the line. If a casualty is unconscious, tie the line to a rescue swimmer.

Drogue/sea anchor—Deploy this immediately you are clear of the stricken vessel. The drogue will improve stability, turn the liferaft entrance away from the wind and waves and slow your rate of drift. Be aware that some drogues deploy automatically.

Waterproof notebook—useful for working out a watch system, keeping a tab of rationing and medication.

Signal card—this shows what the signals from aircraft and ships mean.

Sea survival instructions—a useful reminder of what to do. Supplement them with this book kept in your grab bag.

Radar reflector—deploy this as high as possible. **Do not use with a SART since they can conflict with each other.**

Fishing kit—this gives you something to do. Eat fish if you have plenty of water.

Tin opener—for opening supplies taken from the boat.

Graduated drinking cup—for ensuring fair sharing of water.

Grab bag

The grab bag is designed to supplement the contents of the liferaft. Ideally, it should float and be watertight. The contents should be stowed in waterproof containers that can be opened with cold wet fingers.

Some sailing-yacht racing rules specify what you must have in the grab bag.

Liferaft maintenance:

Different colored sponges
(for bailing and collecting rain water)

Bailer or bucket

Gaffer tape and/
or sail repair tape

Medical:

First Aid Kit

Sea Sickness pills

Sick bags

Dinghy inflatable pump
(more effective than most liferaft pumps)

**Personal items
and protection:**

Sun glasses

Sun cream/block,
lipbalm

Parafoil kite

Sun hat

Warm clothes

Gardening style
leather gloves

Diving mask
or swim goggles

Travelling toothbrush,
toothpaste and
feminine sanitation items

Pack of cards and/
or pocket game

Thermal
protective
aids

Waterproof paper and pen

Chemical
heat packs

GRAB
BAG
FOR
EMERGENCY
USE ONLY

Survival and maintenance items:

- Inflatable cushions
  or cushions grabbed from cabin
- Cutting board
- Drinking water
- Waterproof containers
  (Tupperware' style)
- Torch – self powered
- Food rations
  and food collected from galley
- Bin liners
- Spare batteries
- This Survival Book
- Re-sealable polythene bags
- Cyalume chemical
  light sticks
- Waterproof matches
  (for when you reach shore)
- Tin opener
  for food grabbed from the gall
- Fishing kit
- Scissors
  (with rounded ends)
- Rearming kit for lifejacket s
- Cup with measuring scale

Rescue and navigation:

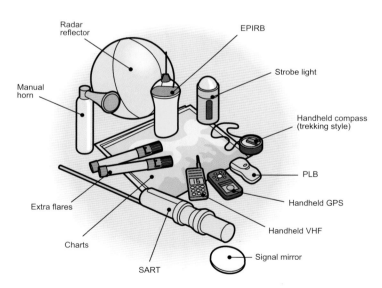

- Radar
  reflector
- EPIRB
- Strobe light
- Manual
  horn
- Handheld compass
  (trekking style)
- PLB
- Handheld GPS
- Extra flares
- Handheld VHF
- Charts
- Signal mirror
- SART

If some items are normally in use on the boat, make up a laminated "grab bag list" of what to take with you. Stow grab bag extras where you know you will be able to find them quickly.

If you have time, take the dinghy as well.

Two-tier system

Pack a fanny pack with small items that will make your eventual return to shore easier: money, credit card, spare spectacles, personal medication, the boat's papers, passports, house- and car-keys, etc. If rescued by helicopter, you will not be able to take a large case with you. It's bad enough losing your boat but not being able to get home, or having to break into your car and house will make it worse.

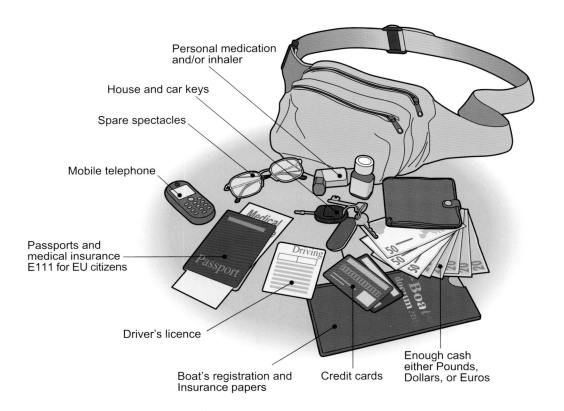

Personal medication and/or inhaler

House and car keys

Spare spectacles

Mobile telephone

Passports and medical insurance E111 for EU citizens

Driver's licence

Boat's registration and Insurance papers

Credit cards

Enough cash either Pounds, Dollars, or Euros

CHAPTER 9 : Fire control

Fire prevention

- Keep the engine bay and electrics clean and tidy
- Install the correct size wiring
- Do not smoke below decks
- Take care with cooking fats and solvents
- Vent the engine compartment (gasoline engines)
- Turn off the gas at source when not needed
- Check the gas system and use a gas alarm
- Ensure all crew know the gas routine
- Fit an automatic extinguisher in the engine compartment

Fire triangle

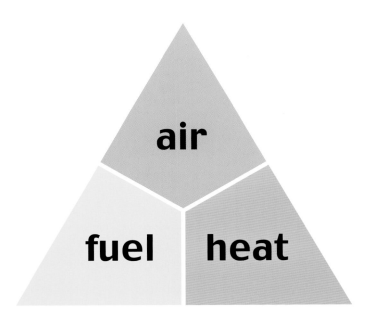

Fires require just three elements to burn. Remove just one of these and the fire will go out.

Fire blanket

Often overlooked but a very useful piece of safety equipment. Use to smother flames on liquid (cooking oil) or people, thereby depriving the fire of air. The blanket also makes a good protective shield when passing close to a fire. DO NOT store directly above a cooker.

Fire extinguishers

All new extinguishers are red with a color-coded area to show the type of extinguishant.

They are rated by the types and size of fire for which they are suitable.

A—carbonaceous (wood, fiberglass, upholstery)
B—flammable liquids
C—flammable gases

Sizes are related to a crib of wood for A-type fires and to a pan of flammable liquid for B-type fires, a typical rating is 5A/34B. The higher the number, the bigger the fire the extinguisher can tackle.

Water (A)
There is plenty of it around (sea)—collect it in a bucket (remembering to first tie a lanyard to the bucket). Water fire extinguishers are available, the water will cool the fire but they are large and heavy. Do not use water on liquid, gas, electrical, or cooking-fat fires.

Dry powder (ABC) Blue
Use on solids, flammable liquid (gasoline/diesel engine fires) and gas fires **but not cooking oil**. It is messy but very effective at knocking down flames, however it is suffocating when used in enclosed spaces, so care must be taken.

AFFF foam (AB) Cream
Use on solids, flammable liquid (gasoline/diesel engine fires) **but not cooking-oil, gas, or electrical fires**. Foam can run off solid objects and allow fire to reignite.

CO_2 (B) Black
Used in manual and automatic extinguishers although not often found on boats. Use on flammable liquid fires but not cooking-oil fires since the blast of gas can cause the oil to splash. **Do not use on people**—expanding gas is cold and can cause severe cold burns.

Automatic extinguishers for engine compartments
Use a single extinguisher of the correct size for the compartment.

Halocarbon gas
A number of environmentally friendly gas extinguishants are now available (FM 200, FE 36) for engine compartments. They are clean to use.

Micro-powder fine powder extinguishant
Chemically reacts with the fire.

Dry-powder (ABC)
Similar to a manual extinguisher. Can be used in naturally aspirated engine compartments. Dry powder will damage engines which have turbo- or super-chargers.

The United States Coast Guard requires the carriage of approved fire extinguishers on all vessels equipped with mechanical propulstion equipment, closed compartments where fuel is stored, or enclosed living spaces.

Position extinguishers at exits from cabins so that they can be used to provide a means of escape. Fire blankets need to be easily accessible but not stored above a cooker. Fit an automatic extinguisher in the engine compartment.

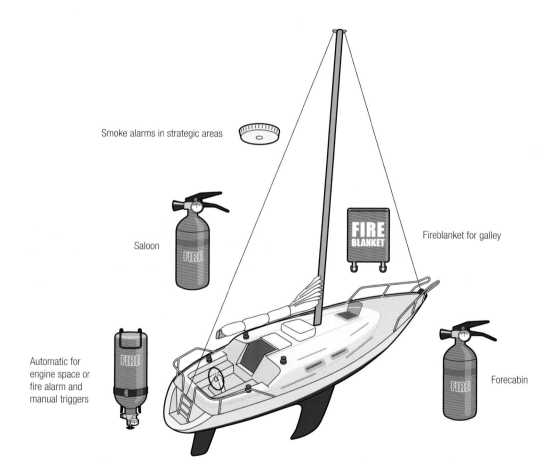

Smoke alarms in strategic areas

Saloon

FIRE BLANKET

Fireblanket for galley

Automatic for engine space or fire alarm and manual triggers

Forecabin

Small extinguishers provide a very limited operating time. A 2.2 lb (1kg) dry powder extinguisher will give about 5 to 6 seconds of extinguisher.

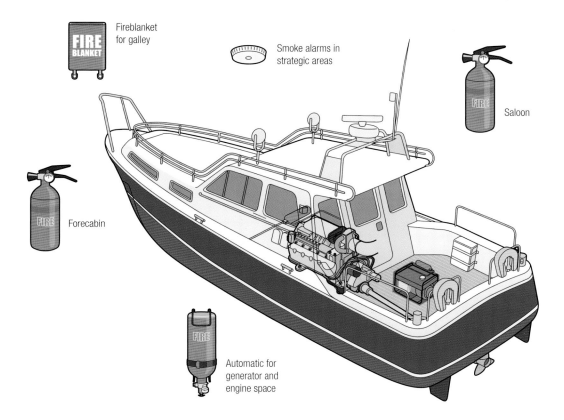

Fireblanket for galley

Smoke alarms in strategic areas

Saloon

Forecabin

Automatic for generator and engine space

Maintenance

Regularly shake dry-powder extinguishers to prevent the powder clumping. Service all extinguishers at the prescribed periods.

Firefighting

Always keep a clear exit behind you when fighting a fire:

Aim the jet from a manual extinguisher at the base of the fire. Keep the extinguisher upright.

Splash rather than throw water. After putting out the fire, use water to cool the area and prevent re-ignition.

Avoid opening the engine compartment hatch unless absolutely necessary. If you have to, crack open the edge of the hatch and fire a manual extinguisher into the compartment.

Protect your hands behind the edges of the fire blanket. Smother clothing using a fire blanket.

If you cannot extinguish the fire, prepare to abandon ship:
- If you are not already wearing lifejackets, put yours on and instruct the crew to do the same
- Send a Mayday
- Use flares
- Launch the liferaft

CHAPTER 10 : Raising the alarm

Are you in distress?

You are in distress when, in the opinion of the skipper, a vessel (boat, yacht, ship), or a person is in grave and imminent danger and requires immediate assistance.

Flares

Flares need to be readily accessible. In a sailing yacht, this usually means just inside the companionway (fig.1) ; in a motor cruiser, beneath or next to the helmsman's seat with some more in the wheelhouse and some on the flybridge (fig. 2). The number and type of flares to carry will depend on where you plan to sail. Race rules often specify a minimum pack that must be carried.

- Stow flares in a waterproof container lined with sponge foam or bubble wrap.
- Do not fasten the container's lid so tightly that others cannot open it.
- Handheld white anti-collision flares need to be immediately available and can be stowed in clips in the companionway or next to the helm. Keep flares out of reach of young children.

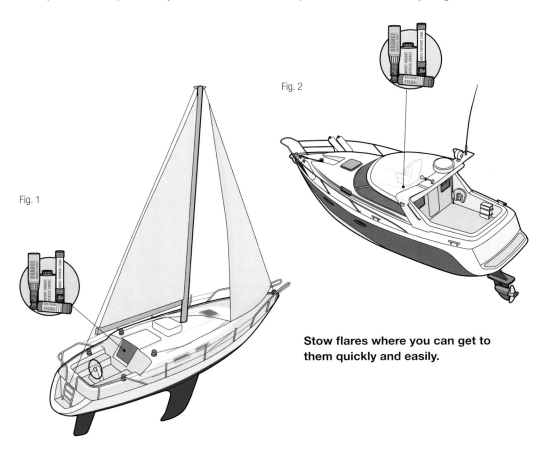

Fig. 2

Fig. 1

Stow flares where you can get to them quickly and easily.

Firing flares

Different makes of flares operate in different ways. Find out how to use your flares before you need them—Read Before You Need!

Which distress flare?

Red handheld flare
Burns for at least one minute at 15,000 candela. Visible up to 7 miles. Use day or night.

Red parachute rocket flare
Fires to a height of 300 meters (328 yards) or more and burns for at least 40 seconds at 30,000 candela. Visible for up to 28 miles. Use day or night.

Handheld orange smoke
Produces bright orange smoke for at least one minute. Visible up to 7 miles. Some handheld smoke flares float and can be used to mark a MOB. Use during daylight only.
Not to SOLAS standard.

Buoyant orange smoke canister
Produces bright-orange smoke for over three minutes. Visible up to 7 miles. Use during daylight only. Can be used to mark a MOB.

Day/night flare
Personal flare, waterproof. Used by divers and RNLI crew. Has a smoke flare at one end and a red flare at the other. Each end burns for 18 to 20 seconds. Visible up to 7 miles.
Not to SOLAS standard.

Mini-flare
Personal aerial flare fires up to a height of 60 meters (65 yards). Comes with up to ten cartridges. Burns for up to 8 seconds. Fire two cartridges in succession. Visible up to 15 miles at night, 10 miles during day. **Not to SOLAS standard.**

Aerial distress flares raise the alarm. Handheld distress flares can be used to raise the alarm but also to pinpoint your position.

Fire all flares with your back to the wind. Find a firm footing before operating the flare.

Parachute rocket flares reach a height of over 300 yards. For low cloud conditions it may be possible to fire the flare at an angle so that it deploys under the clouds. Orange smoke flares help to pinpoint your position.

Firing a parachute rocket flare:

1. Brace yourself in a firm position
2. Back to the wind
3. Remove any caps or covers
4. Check aloft to make sure it's clear of obstructions such as rigging, the flybridge, or helicopters
5. Note which way up the flare needs to be fired
6. Remove the safety pin (if fitted)
7. Grip the flare firmly about two-thirds of the way up, the flare will recoil when fired
8. Gently squeeze the trigger upwards until the flare fires
9. Rocket flares tend to seek the wind. If the cloud level is low, fire at an angle downwind so that the flare ignites below cloud

Handheld flares

Hold handheld flares over the leeward side at an angle of 45 degrees to prevent hot ash or burning material from damaging the boat or liferaft. Leather (gardening) gloves can be worn to protect the hands. Flares do not extinguish in water. If you drop a flare it will quickly burn through a liferaft or even a fiberglass or wooden hull.

Buoyant orange smokes are activated and then dropped into the sea on the leeward side of the boat or raft to build up a cloud of smoke.

Non-distress flares

Handheld white flares raise awareness and pinpoint your position to other shipping to prevent collision.

White parachute rocket flare

Used to illuminate the local area at night. Good for searching for MOB.

GMDSS

The Global Maritime Distress and Safety System was fully implemented in February 1999. It provides an International co-ordinated approach to calling for help and requires merchant vessels to carry at least two independent means of radio distress alerting. Leisure craft carry calling equipment voluntarily. It also provides for urgency and safety communications and for the provision of navigational and weather warnings.

The type of equipment suggested depends on where you sail. GMDSS divides the world into four areas:
Area A1—within range of a shore-based VHF Coast Station fitted with DSC (up to 50 miles depending on antenna height).
Area A2—within range of a shore-based MF Coast Station fitted with DSC (up to between 100 and 300 miles).
Area A3—between latitudes 70 degrees N and 70 degrees S.
Area A4—north of 70 degrees N and south of 70 degrees S (the polar regions).

Equipment covered by GMDSS includes—VHF, MF/HF SSB (radio tranceivers), Inmarsat A/B, C and M (satellite communications systems), Navtex, EPIRBs, PLBs, and SARTs.

Raising the alarm

Mayday is the internationally
recognized word to indicate distress.

DSC—Digital Selective Calling is a
major part of the GMDSS. In a matter
of seconds, pressing one button
(correctly) will alert the rescue services
and other shipping in the vicinity. The
alert will tell them who you are, where
you are and that you need help. DSC
should also reduce routine radio traffic
on Ch 16 making it easier to hear
voice distress calls.

Using a VHF DSC radio

Make sure the radio is switched on and receiving position information from GPS. Different makes
of radio transceiver operate in slightly different ways but the general approach shown below will
operate most sets. However, make sure everyone on board knows how the radio works.

Lift the cover over the distress button and press and release the distress button once. This will
(usually) provide a menu of types of distress.

If there's time, select the type of distress that suits your circumstances.

Press and hold the distress button again for five seconds (the radio will count down) until the call
is sent. The radio may sound an alarm. Press CLR to stop the audio alarm. The radio will switch
automatically to Ch 16. Make your voice Mayday call.

DSC distress calls will be sent automatically every four minutes, for as long as the radio can do so,
until an acknowledgment is received.

Mayday by voice

Non-DSC VHF radios will need to be manually switched to Ch 16. Press the Ch 16 button and check that the radio is switched to high power. If not, push the H/L or 1/25 button.

Now make your voice Mayday call.

A reminder card next to the radio can help to make sure the right information is transmitted. In the panic of the moment it's easy to make mistakes. Try to speak slowly.

MAYDAY MAYDAY MAYDAY

THIS IS... yacht name spoken three times.

DSC—say your MMSI number.

MAYDAY... yacht name

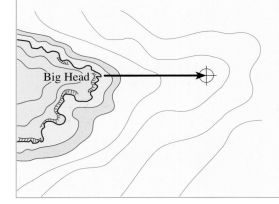

POSITION IS... give position in either Lat and Long or distance and bearing from a charted object

NATURE OF DISTRESS—describe briefly what the problem is, for example, sinking, MOB, boat on fire, stranded, broken down close to rocky lee shore, etc.

I REQUIRE IMMEDIATE ASSISTANCE

NUMBER OF PEOPLE ON BOARD— don't forget to include yourself

FURTHER INFORMATION—anything else that may help rescuers, such as abandoning to liferaft, triggered EPIRB or PLB etc.

OVER—the invitation to reply

You should receive a digital acknowledgment from the rescue services or ship, followed by a voice reply. If no acknowledgment or voice reply is received, check the batteries are on, the set is switched on and that Ch 16 and high power are selected. Repeat the procedure.

If still no reply, try a voice call on another Channel—Ch 6 or, if you are in shipping lanes, Ch 13. Prefixing the boat's name with the words "Yacht" or "Motor Cruiser" helps rescuers know what they are looking for.

VHF versus cell phone

A cell phone can be used to call for help but is a poor substitute for a marine VHF radio, the reasons being:

- VHF radios have a greater range.
- They raise the alarm with all in range who are listening.
- SAR services can determine and home in on VHF transmission, they have a longer battery life and can send distress calls in seconds (DSC).
- Cell phones are designed for land use.
- They have poor coverage at sea and reduced range.
- They only alert the person you call. But in a real emergency a cell phone is better than nothing.
- The emergency services operator will be the first one available and maybe located anywhere in the country.

Use the National Emergency Services number: in the US, dial 911, (dial 112 throughout Europe, 999 in the UK) and ask for the Coast Guard.

Satellite mobile phones

Satellite phones are becoming a popular alternative to SSB radio.

In January 2006, experienced yachtsman Richard Wood and his partner Jetti were on passage from Nicaragua to Mexico aboard his catamaran *Eclipse* when they were caught in stormforce conditions. Wave heights were estimated at approaching 30ft with winds of over 70 knots. The sea anchor had been torn to shreds and they tried running downwind trailing warps and anchors but there was increasing danger of capsize. By late afternoon they decided they needed to call for help before things got worse and so set off their EPIRB and telephoned HM Coastguard in Falmouth (Cornwall, England) on their satellite telephone. The HM Coastguard contacted the Mexican authorities. Mr. Woods continued to telephone the HM Coastguard every hour to check on progress and give a position and weather update. At 11pm, a helicopter from the USS *Ford* contacted *Eclipse* and the pair were lifted to safety.

Other Distress signals

Raising and lowering outstretched arms

Continuous sounding of horn

Morse SOS by light

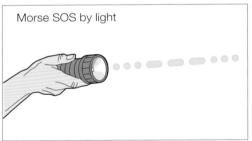

Black ball over a black square

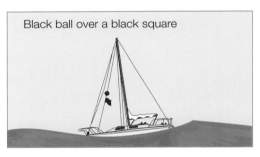

Smoke

Code flags N over C

Upside down ensign

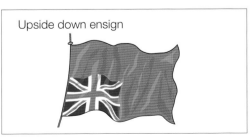

Divers

A diver on the surface will indicate distress by waving. They may also have raised their goggles onto the top of their head. Don't simply wave back and sail by—they are asking for help.

Using a heliograph (mirror or CD)

A heliograph is a simple way of drawing attention. Some come with a short stick and string but you can also use your hand. Using two fingers as a sight, reflect the light onto the two fingers. The target will then see the reflection off the mirror. Practice with a CD but be aware that its shiny surface will dissolve in water.

Need help but you are not in distress

You can also ask for assistance by making a Pan Pan call on the radio preceded by an Urgency Alert on DSC (if fitted).

By Voice

PAN PAN (Three times)

ALL SHIPS (Three times)

THIS IS... name of boat x 3 (+ MMSI if fitted with DSC)

POSITION IS... give position in either Latitude and Longditude or distance and bearing from a charted object

NATURE OF PROBLEM I am broken down and require a tow

NO. OF PERSONS ON BOARD don't forget to include yourself

OVER

Let the SAR authorities know as soon as something goes wrong. Don't wait until the last minute.

Code flag V indicates "I require assistance."

EPIRBs

An Emergency Position Indicating Radio Beacon will alert the Rescue Services by sending a distress signal via satellites. Two sets of satellites pick up the signals: Inmarsat and Cospas-Sarsat. Inmarsat satellites are in geostationary orbit. Cospas-Sarsat satellites are in a lower polar orbit and circle the earth approximately every 12 hours.

There are two types of EPIRB: standard and GPS. Both transmit a signal on 406MHz, which includes an identification code.

GPS-enabled EPIRBs also transmit position information that Inmarsat satellites will immediately download to an Earth station. The position information may come from a built-in receiver or from a link to the vessel's own GPS receiver.

Standard EPIRBs' positions are found using Doppler Frequency Shift theory by Cospas-Sarsat satellites. They require two satellite passes before an approximate position can be found. Each satellite will hold and then download data as soon as a ground station comes into range.

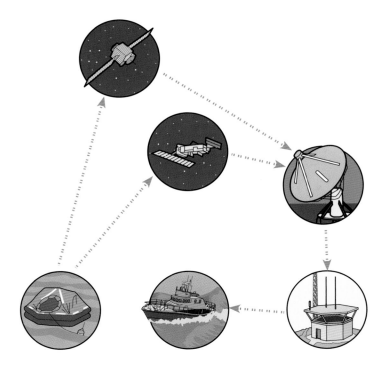

When the EPIRB is activated, it transmits a signal via satellite to an Earth station. The Earth station sends it to the appropriate rescue coordination center, who will task a ship or local rescue services to your position.

GPS EPIRB—provides a distress alert immediately and a position within five minutes accurate to 100 yards.

Standard EPIRB—provides a distress alert immediately, if the Earth station is within the satellite range, and a position to within 3 nautical miles (5km) within 40 to 120 minutes depending on your location. EPIRBs can be activated manually or automatically on contact with the sea. Float-free versions are also available. Built to SOLAS standards, they have a battery life of 48 hours and will float upright.

Also built into the EPIRB is a 121.5MHz homing beacon and SAR craft use radio direction finders to home into the signal.

All 406MHz EPIRBs are required to be registered in the country of their vessel's flag. These details are used to check the authenticity of a distress alert. Batteries need to be replaced at the manufacturer's required date. Check the instructions and make a note of the date they need to be replaced—always replace the batteries.

PLBs

Personal Locator Beacons, sometimes referred to as PEPIRBs, are similar to EPIRBs but they are smaller and are designed to be worn by an individual crew member. Most countries require 406MHz PLBs to be registered.

As with EPIRBs, there are two 406MHz PLB types. Both operate with the Inmarsat and Cospas-Sarsat satellites in the same way as EPIRBs:

- GPS PLB—provides a distress alert immediately and a position within five minutes accurate to 100 yards.

- Standard PLB—provides distress alert immediately and a position to within 3 nautical miles (5km) within 40 to 120 minutes depending on your location.

Also built into the PLB is a 121.5MHz homing beacon. SAR craft use radio direction finders to home into the signal.

Unlike EPIRBs, PLBs do not float upright. They have a battery life of 24 hours and can only be activated manually.

121.5 PLBs

Designed to be worn by individual crew members, 121.5 PLBs can trigger an onboard alarm to warn crew that somebody has gone over the side. A radio direction finder can also be used to home in on the MOB. Always tell the SAR services if a MOB may be using a 121.5 PLB.

The MOB should hold the antenna as high as possible to give the greatest range.

MOB alerting devices

Proprietary MOB alerting devices that work on non-SAR rescue frequencies are also available. Some are capable of being linked to the GPS MOB button or an autopilot or may come with an appropriate radio direction finder.

RNLI MOB Guardian

This is a new worldwide system, developed by the UK-based Royal National Lifeboat Institution, which continually monitors boat and crew. An onboard transceiver sends regular position and condition data updates via the Iridium satellite system to the RNLI Operations Center. If data is not received, the RNLI alerts the local rescue coordination center to the vessel's last known position.

The transceiver also includes personal proximity alarms to be worn by each crew member. If crew goes out of range of the transceiver, it activates an alarm and alerts the RNLI Operations Center.

SARTs

A Search-and-Rescue Radar Transponder is an alert and position-finding electronic device that produces a distinctive "echo" on the screen of any 9GHz Radar. Previously only used on commercial vessels' liferafts, SARTs are now available sufficiently small enough to be fitted as an optional extra in most leisure liferafts.

Fig. 1   **Fig. 2**   **Fig. 3**

On initial contact with a SART, the radar shows a line of dots giving the range and direction of the casualty (fig. 1). As the radar closes on the SART, the dots broaden to arcs (fig. 2). When the arcs make an almost complete circle the SART is within 1 mile (fig. 3).

Range will depend on the height of the SART and the height of the Radar scanner. A SAR helicopter at (3000ft can pick up a SART 48 miles away. A radar scanner 7 yards above the waterline will "see" a SART at about 6 miles.

The SART starts transmitting when it receives a radar signal. Switch off your vessel's radar before abandoning ship, to prevent your SART from transmitting before rescuers are in range.

Position the SART as high as possible to achieve the greatest range.

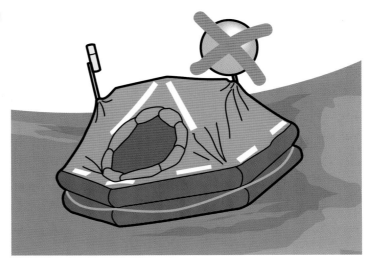

**SARTs and inflatable radar reflectors conflict—
use only one at a time.**

CHAPTER 11 : When to abandon ship

There are two main reasons to abandon ship:

1. If your boat sinks
2. If your boat catches fire and the fire cannot be controlled

If there is no grave danger of the boat immediately sinking, then stay with your boat because:

- It carries far more supplies than your liferaft
- It will probably offer better shelter from the elements
- You may be able to find a way to jury-rig a repair and improve your conditions
- It makes a much larger target for rescuers to see

Your boat is full of supplies—only leave it if it sinks or catches fire. It makes a much bigger target for rescuers to find compared to a liferaft, a huddle of survivors, a single person with a lifejacket and/or a dan buoy or a person without a lifejacket.

What you need to survive

To ensure your survival you need the correct equipment with the right knowledge and, most importantly, a belief and will to survive. The four tenets of survival are protection, location, water, and food. To this end, the survivor requires:

Equipment
- Personal survival aids
- Life-saving appliances
- Grab bag

Knowledge
- What equipment you have
- How to use it properly
- Have a strategy ready

Will to Survive
- Believe you will be rescued
- Avoid blame
- Positive attitude

I will survive!

The greatest factor in any survival situation is the positive mental attitude of the would-be survivor, some call it the will to survive. There are numerous examples where a sheer determination not to be beaten, to keep going despite the odds has made the difference between life and death. The belief that, no matter how bad the situation, you will pull through has to be emphasized to every casualty; a liferaft or semi-submerged boat is no place for negative thinking.

Obviously, a will to survive is not enough on its own. Training, preparation and a good understanding of the factors that will affect your survival will bolster that belief. Positive leadership will also improve a crew's chances of survival.

Be aware that tiredness, cold, seasickness, and injury add to demoralizing a crew and that the loss or death of a crew member can have devastating effects on the survivors' will to live.

Tony Bullimore's 60-foot yacht capsized in 60-knot winds in the Southern Ocean when it lost its keel during the Vendée Globe single-handed round-the-world race in January 1997, 1700 miles from Perth, Western Australia.

Without a keel, the boat remained inverted (upside down) with Bullimore caught inside the hull, waist-deep in water. Realizing that he would have sufficient air to breathe and that the boat was unlikely to sink, he assessed his situation and put together a survival strategy.

He activated his EPIRB knowing that help would take several days to reach him. Although he was wearing a drysuit, he realized that he had to get out of the freezing water. In total darkness, he managed to jury-rig a hammock from cargo nets. He was aware that spotter planes may not

realize that he was still alive inside the hull so he made several attempts to swim out of the cabin to release his liferaft so that it would float free next to the yacht. Each attempt sapped his strength and resulted in two hours of intense shivering back in his hammock. But his will to survive forced him to keep trying. For four days he lived on limited supplies of water and chocolate. The Royal Australian Navy rescued him, hypothermic and dehydrated but alive.

When disaster strikes

Crew will probably react in one of three ways when a yacht founders:

- 10 to 20% will remain calm and be aware of the situation and will respond appropriately
- 75% will be stunned and bewildered, they will be unable to judge what to do for the best and be unable to concentrate on a task
- 10 to 15% will react inappropriately and may not realise the seriousness of their predicament, they may scream, weep or be unable to move

Applied to a crew of six, these figures suggest that there will be;

- one person who is able to react effectively
- four who will need goading to undertake tasks
- one who may completely lose touch with reality and could endanger themself or their colleagues

A good leader, who may or may not be the skipper, will stay positive, prevent recriminations, take stock of the situation, and organize and allocate tasks to the survivors. Good planning and preparation, training, and knowledge of what to expect will increase the number of crew who react appropriately.

CHAPTER 12 : Abandoning ship

Don't leave your boat until your boat leaves you! It is packed full of supplies and useful equipment that will aid your survival.

A few tasks, carried out before you abandon, may save your boat: emptying water tanks, therefore turning them into buoyancy tanks, closing the engine-cooling-water seacock, and disconnecting the raw-water feed, and using the engine-cooling system to pump out the bilge.

Drills for abandoning ship

Prior to abandonment

1. Make everybody aware that you are preparing to abandon ship. **Stay calm.**

2. Activate the EPIRB. Press DSC distress button on VHF / HF radio. Make a voice distress call.

3. Fire parachute rockets if someone is likely to be within 30 miles.

4. Get everyone on board to put on layers of warm clothing. Extra clothing will not weigh you down in the water. Initially, it will help you float.

5. Waterproof clothing will reduce cold-water shock and heat-sapping water flow around your body. Use an immersion suit. **Keeping warm is a priority.**

6. Check everyone has donned lifejackets correctly—use a buddy system to speed things up. Inflate lifejackets before entering the water.

7. Have a drink (non-alcoholic) and take anti-seasickness tablets.

8. Find the grab bag and as many useful extras as you can lay your hands on.

9. Standby to launch the liferaft in case the vessel has to be abandoned quickly.

Priorities are donning lifejackets, sending Mayday, initiating the EPIRB and launching the liferaft. Anything else is a bonus.

Do not launch the liferaft earlier than you need it because it is difficult to hold a raft alongside in a rough sea.

Launching and entering liferaft

Prior to launching the liferaft

1. Secure the painter to a strongpoint—
   ask another crew member to check the
   knot. A round turn and two half-hitches
   is sufficient but any knot that holds will do.

2. Check that the water is clear of debris or
   the raft may be damaged as soon as it
   inflates.

3. Launch the liferaft to the leeward
   (downwind) side of boat.

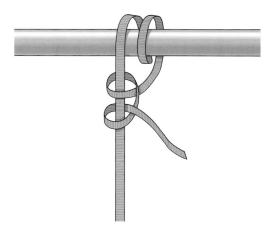

Liferafts are heavy and difficult to manhandle—a six-man raft can weigh between 55lbs (25kg)
and 165lbs (75kg) depending on its quality, type and contents. Launch them from as near to the
stowage site as possible. It may need two people to lift the liferaft canister.

Launch the raft to leeward

Launching the raft to leeward will provide some protection from the prevailing conditions when
boarding it.

The freeboard is likely to be lower on the leeward side, making the raft easier to board and
reducing the chances of the raft damaging itself on the side of the boat.

However, you may have to move the raft to a safer position—for example, because of a fire. Take care not to slip and injure yourself or lose yourself or the raft overboard. Be aware of other dangers such as flogging sails.

Launching the liferaft

4. Pull the painter. It's likely to be up to 33ft (10 meters) long.
5. When the painter is fully extended, a sharp tug will trigger the gas inflation mechanism.
6. The raft will inflate in 30 to 60 seconds.

You may hear gas escaping during and shortly after inflation. This is excess CO_2 being expelled through the pressure-relief valves and is normal.

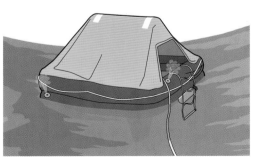

Launching the liferaft to windward may make it more difficult to board. Sharp barnacles on the bottom of the boat may puncture the liferaft tubes.

Don't let the liferaft drift away. In strong winds it may be too difficult to pull it or even winch it back to the boat, leaving you with no raft.

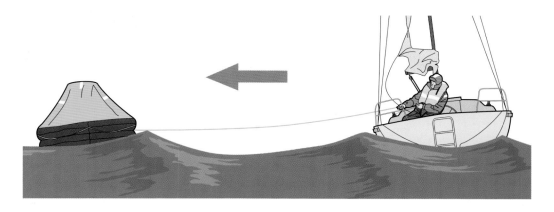

If the raft inflates upside down or capsizes before you can board it, try to right it while still onboard the vessel.

STAY OUT OF THE WATER—COLD KILLS

Boarding the liferaft

Remove sharp objects before entering the raft from your person such as keys attached to a belt clip.

Try to climb directly into the liferaft from the boat. The strongest and heaviest person should board the raft first to stabilize it and to help others in. As each person gets in they should move out of the way of the entrance and balance the raft as the others board.

Avoid jumping if at all possible. You risk injuring yourself or others already in the raft. Do not jump onto the canopy. If you have to jump, the maximum recommended height is 6 feet.

Spread the impact load by holding your feet slightly apart and your arms out.

REMEMBER TO LOAD THE GRAB BAG AND EXTRAS

Leave any injured to the last but one. If they enter early, other people may make their injuries worse if they land on them. Get the injured aboard the raft before the last able person leaves the boat.

Entering the water

Only enter the water if you are unable to board the raft direct from the boat.

If possible, enter the water slowly, either by lowering yourself on a rope or by using the boat's fixed or emergency boarding ladder, this will minimize the effects of cold-water shock.

If a slow entry is not possible:

1. Go to the side of the boat where the freeboard is least or upwind of fire and smoke.

2. Steady yourself and check below for debris and other people.

3. Inflate your lifejacket.

4. Place one arm over the top of the lifejacket to prevent it from jumping up when you enter the water.

5. Use your other hand to cover your airway.

6. Look ahead to stop you from toppling forward—check the area is clear and step off the side of boat.

7. Put your feet together and enter the water in an upright position.

8. Hold this position until you have surfaced and regained control of your breathing.

At night or in heavy weather, it may be prudent to clip your safety harness to the liferaft painter and pull yourself along it until you reach the raft.

While waiting to get into the raft, hook your arm through the lifelines fixed around the outside of the raft. Cold, numb hands will be unable to grip the lifeline. Do not let go until you are onboard the raft.

Getting into the liferaft from the water

The cumbersome shape of an inflated lifejacket, the weight of wet clothing and the strength-sapping effects of cold water make it very difficult to climb unaided into a liferaft from the water. The strongest and fittest person should enter the raft first. They can then help others to board.

All liferafts have ramps or ladders to aid entry. Get a foothold on the ladder and a firm grip on the handhold on top or just inside the top tube.

Partially deflating your lifejacket may make it easier to reach handholds inside the raft, especially if wearing a 275N lifejacket.

Rescuing survivors

Get casualties into the raft quickly. The two strongest survivors should be on either side of the entrance and grab hold of the casualty's lifejacket straps and pull them face-first up and into the raft.

GET EVERYONE OUT OF THE WATER FAST.

Make sure that semi-conscious casualties are not lying face-down in the water in the bottom of the raft. Look out for flailing legs.

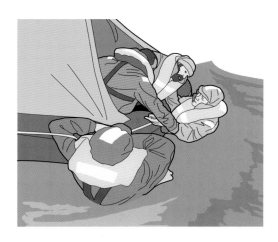

Once you are in the raft, move to the opposite side to help keep the raft balanced.

Keep a count of survivors. Continually check that none drift away. Communicate with those in the water. Help each other.

Pulling casualties in backwards by using their inherent buoyancy and dunking them first is slow and difficult and may also injure their back.

Righting a capsized raft

With the correct technique, one person can right any raft with a capacity of up to 12 persons.

Whenever possible right the liferaft while still on the boat

1. Using the lifelines, move around the outside of the raft to the gas bottle. There should be a sign or symbol saying "right here."

2. Reach up and find the line or webbing handles on the bottom of the raft.

3. Pull yourself up on the edge of the raft.

4. Draw up your knees and place them in the fold of the tubes. Use them as a fulcrum. Lean back while holding on the righting line.

5. Pull the raft over on top of you. It's much easier if you can get the wind underneath the raft as you begin to lift.

6. Hold on to the line and stay on your back. As the raft comes over, keep your hand up to create an air pocket under the raft.

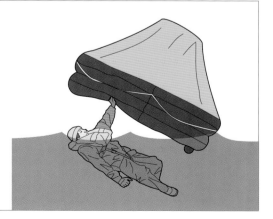

7. Use the line to pull and guide yourself out from under the raft. Mind your head on the gas bottle.

8. Do not let go of the raft. If the wind catches it, it will be blown away faster than you can swim.

9. Do not turn on to your front when under the raft. The buoyancy in the lifejacket will trap you against the floor.

Note that self-righting rafts are also available.

Initial actions

- Cut the painter with the buoyant safety knife (held in a sheath close to the liferaft entrance).

- Cut it as close to the point of attachment to the boat as possible.

- Pull in the line, it may prove to be useful later.

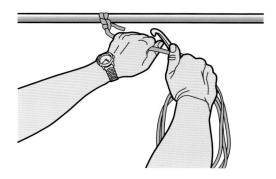

- Paddle clear of the sinking or burning vessel to prevent the raft from becoming damaged.

- Pick up other survivors from the water.

- Congregate with other liferafts and fasten them together.

- Salvage anything that might be useful.

- Stream the sea anchor when you are clear of the vessel. It will turn the raft's entrance away from the wind and waves. It will also improve the raft's stability and slow its rate of drift, keeping you closer to the area where the rescuers will be searching.

- Retrieve the canister lid and any packaging.

- Pick up any useful flotsam.

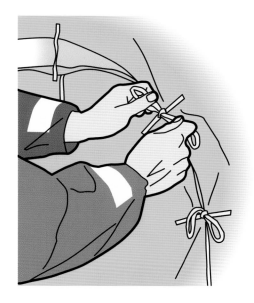

Close the raft's entrance to prevent further ingress of wind and water. It will also keep the warmth in. Entrance closures range from heavy-duty zips to Velcro fastening to webbing ties. Make sure that, whichever system is used, the raft entrance can be opened quickly. Use slipknots on ties.

Open the entrance every 20 minutes to allow fresh air in. Most pressure-relief valves vent outside the raft. If the PRVs vent inside the raft, open the door to let out the fumes. Inhaling CO_2 will give you a headache.

Maintain the raft by checking for leaks and bailing out. Check that the equipment pack is still secured inside the raft, if not check outside the raft; it may still be afloat and retrievable.

Remember...

1. CUT the painter

2. STREAM the sea anchor

3. CLOSE the door

4. MAINTAIN the raft

Secondary actions

What to do next

Be aware that there will be a great temptation to collapse into the liferaft and relax. Now's not the time to rest. Get organized before the cold saps your strength and your ability to use your hands.

If anti-seasickness medication has not been taken before boarding the raft, open the liferaft pack, find anti-seasickness tablets and take them now. Everyone must take one. Even the hardiest of sailors is likely to be sick inside a raft.

Be prepared—take out one or two seasickness bags as well. Once someone is sick, everyone else is likely to be affected.

Seasickness will cause not only physical and psychological debility but also loss of valuable body heat and fluid. It may also mean the sufferer loses their medication before it takes effect.

The priority now is to get as warm and as dry as possible.

Bail out the raft. The bailer provided may be no more than a fabric scoop. Some rafts have a self-bailer fitted in the floor that will drain the water automatically.

If not, bail out by hand using the bailer and other containers—a boot, a bucket or the salvaged liferaft canister lid. Use the portable bilge pump from your grab bag. Be resourceful.

Use one of the sponges from the liferaft pack to dry the floor of the raft. Remember to keep another sponge clean for fresh-water collection.

Apply first-aid to those that require it. Everyone is likely to be suffering from varying degrees of hypothermia and shock in addition to injuries. Look out for the quiet ones—the quietest casualties are likely to be the worst-injured. Calm those that are acting inappropriately.

Collect sharp objects and weapons—knives, multi-tools etc.—that could damage the raft or be used to harm or threaten anyone when rations become short and tempers fray at a later date.

Wring out wet clothing and put it back on. Huddle together for warmth—don't be shy!

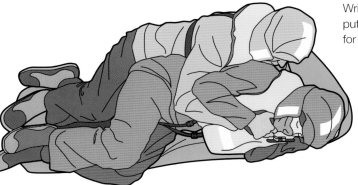

Your main heat loss is by conduction through the raft floor. Some floors have thermally reflective surfaces but others need to be inflated with the bellows. Take care not to pump water into the floor. Insulation can also be provided by sitting on salvaged bunk cushions, fenders or, conditions permitting, inflated lifejackets.

ISAF, ISO 9650 Part 1: Type 1 and SOLAS raft packs include a number of TPAs (thermal protective aids) that will reduce the body's evaporative heat losses. Thick plastic bags, large bin liners or the salvaged liferaft polythene wrapping could also be used.

KEEP YOUR HEAD WARM.

Locate the pressure-relief valve stoppers and put them in place to prevent leakage through the valves. Check for leaks. Top up the tubes with the pump if necessary. Repair kits will only work if you can dry the area to be repaired. Use liferaft repair clamps if the hole is large, and then reinflate the tube.

A leader, who may not be the skipper, will emerge. It may be the fittest person with the most sea survival knowledge. Their job is to make sure everyone believes they are going to be rescued and to organize the crew and resources effectively.

It's important that everyone works as part of a team to increase the chances of survival and keep each other's morale up.

No recriminations—there will be plenty of time for that after you've been rescued.

THE WILL TO SURVIVE IS PARAMOUNT.
KEEP MORALE HIGH.

Read the survival notes in the liferaft instruction booklet to refresh your memory. Stow equipment that needs to be kept dry in resealable bags. Some rafts will have stowage pockets on the canopy tube high above the water.

Establish a routine as soon as possible. If there are sufficient crew, put two people on watch for between 20 minutes and 2 hours depending on the weather conditions. Make sure the watch system is fair.

Outside watch should keep a lookout for ships, aircraft, other survivors and dangers. They must be fully briefed on signalling with flares, heliograph and VHF.

Inside watch should keep the raft inflated, treat and look after casualties, collect water, bail out, etc.

Switch off the liferaft light during the day to preserve its power. It may seem very dim but to an SAR helicopter's or lifeboat's night-vision goggles it will stand out for miles. Switch off and save lifejacket lights—you may be able to use them when the liferaft light fails.

SOLAS rafts have an inflatable radar reflector. Wetting the canopy may also increase the radar reflection range.

Do not use a radar reflector and SART at the same time.

Look after the handheld VHF, EPIRB, PLB, and flares since they are probably your best means of location by rescuers. Save the VHF's batteries—remember its range is limited. If conditions allow, stand up when using the VHF to increase its range.

Avoid urine retention because it could have serious consequences later. Urinate within two hours of boarding. Female survivors may prefer to use the bailer. Take care not to fall in if urinating out of the entrance. Ask other survivors to hold your lifejacket straps.

You cannot reabsorb urine from the bladder. Urinating will not increase your rate of dehydration. Try to get rid of urine overboard. The smell can cause nausea. Avoid urinating in your clothes since cross-infection could cause problems later.

A bowel movement is not uncommon. You will probably not need to do it again if you are not ingesting food or fluid.

Protection

In northern European and southern Australian waters, the cold is your greatest enemy. The liferaft is designed to help save you from drowning and reduce heat loss by getting you out of the water as well as providing protection from wind chill.

As long as the canopy is providing a good seal from wind and waves, the air inside the raft will be warmed by the body heat of the occupants. Therefore the greatest heat loss is from conduction through the floor of the raft.

Dry the raft floor thoroughly. Pools of water will intensify conductive heat loss. Inflatable floors will need considerable air pressure before providing an air gap beneath seated survivors. Better insulation may be provided by sitting on lifejackets, fenders, bunk cushions or anything else you have salvaged. Only remove your lifejackets if conditions allow and you are confident that the raft is stable.

Put on a hat, raise your hood, cover your head with a scarf or other fabric. Your head loses more heat than any other part of your body.

Once you are insulated from the water, the greatest heat loss will be due to evaporation of water from wet clothes. To stop this, remove and wring dry your clothes. Put the damp clothes back on and don a thermal protective aid (TPA).

TPAs reduce evaporative heat losses by containing the water vapor in the bag. Once the air inside the bag reaches saturation, no more water can be absorbed and evaporation stops. If TPAs are not available, use bin liners or plastic sheeting.

Reflective blankets are not effective in a cold, wet environment. Radiant heat losses from a cold casualty are minimal and the blanket's reflectivity is reduced to virtually nothing as water vapor condenses on its cool inner surface.

Survival or immersion suits are for extreme conditions and provide the best protection against cold. They tend to be bulky and awkward to put on, particularly in a hurry in a confined space, however many people have survived by using one.

Water and food rationing

For survival, the human body needs water more than food. Tests have shown that a person will live for only seven to ten days without water assuming there is no excessive fluid loss but can survive for 20 to 30 days without food.

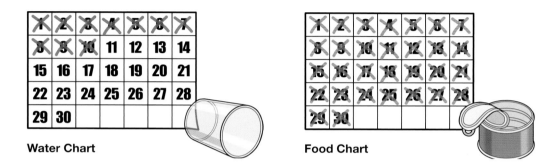

Water Chart

Food Chart

In busy waterways such as those found in northern Europe, it is unlikely a raft will be adrift for more than 48 hours before being rescued. The greatest dangers are drowning and hypothermia rather than dehydration or starvation.

Since the human body has a reserve of water and energy within its tissues, no food or water should be taken in the first 24 hours except by children or conscious injured casualties, who will experience greater fluid loss.

If only minimal water supplies are available, the ration for water, after 24 hours, is half a liter per person per day. (0.5lt/person/day = just under 1 pint/person/day)

Take a third of a ration at sunrise, a third at midday and a third at sunset. When drinking water, keep it in your mouth for as long as possible to moisten the membranes.

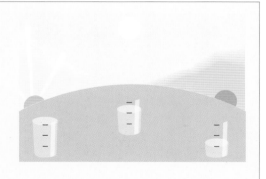

To maintain morale and good harmony, it is vital to ensure that food and water rations are issued fairly.

Water may be supplied in the liferaft pack. It will be in sealed sachets. Use the scissors in the first-aid kit and open the sachet carefully. Decant any leftover water into a clean bottle or sealable container. Stow an empty bottle in your grab bag to collect leftover water.

If you have plenty of water, each person may drink up to 1 liter per day.
(1lt/person/day = about 2 pints/person/day)

Whether you have plenty or virtually none, start to collect water from the outset—you don't know when it might rain again.

Drink collected water first—because bottled water and sealed-sachet water will stay fresh for longer than rainwater.

Do not drink urine. Do not drink seawater, even in a diluted state. Death has been found to occur quicker when you drink seawater rather than nothing at all.

Reduce the body's water loss by making the best use of the shade and cooling from the breeze.

Avoid eating protein-based food (such as fish or meat) because digesting them uses more fluid than they provide. Carbohydrates and sugars are better.

On July 30th 1945, the USS *Indianapolis* was attacked by a Japanese submarine. The ship sank in 12 minutes and many survivors ended up in the water. Rescuers took several days to reach them. Desperately thirsty, some survivors drank seawater.

They became delirious and started to hallucinate. Some thought that there was an island nearby and would try to swim off to it. Some claimed

that the ship was not sunk but was just below the surface and convinced others to remove their lifejackets and swim down with them to drink from a water fountain.

Of a crew of 1,196, it's estimated 900 went into the water. Four days later, only 316 men remained alive. While some were lost to sharks, many were lost due to the effects of drinking seawater.

Long-term survival techniques

Sustaining the will to survive and the belief that you will be rescued is essential. Keep the survivors' morale high by running a disciplined routine. Fear, panic, despair, and recriminations will undermine your belief that you will pull through. Knowledge of survival techniques and confidence in equipment will help you remain calm and positive.

Lack of water and food will cause fatigue and exhaustion and increase depression. Catching food can be a great morale-booster and will supply much-needed energy. Rest as much as you can but when you are not asleep, keep busy with routine raft duties. Stay optimistic and look forward to the future. Discuss what you plan to do when you get ashore.

Long-term survival techniques revolve around collecting or making water to drink, fishing, keeping the raft inflated and in good order and keeping watch for potential rescuers.

> COLLECT RAINWATER AT EVERY OPPORTUNITY.

Better-quality liferafts have a small rain-catcher fitted to the canopy of the raft. It's important to prepare the canopy and the collection bottle before the rain arrives. Wash built-up salt crystals off the canopy and rinse containers with fresh seawater. Use the first downpour to wash off the remaining salt—anything you collect during the initial shower will be contaminated and undrinkable. Collect the rainwater once the salt has been washed off.

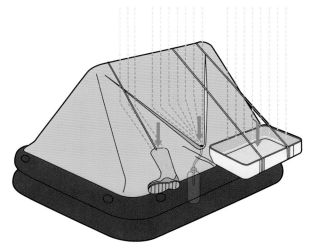

Improvise other means of collecting rainwater—the canopy's collection system is not large.

Unpalatable rainwater can be ingested by enema. Lyn Robertson, a qualified nurse, used the raft's bellows as a method for introducing poor-quality rainwater for absorption through the gut on her family when they were shipwrecked for 37 days in June 1972.

However, tests have shown that saltwater enemas are not a solution to dehydration. The gut does not filter salt out of the water—only use rainwater.

Solar still

An inflatable solar still can be filled and fastened alongside the raft. Salt water held in the bottom of the still evaporates and potable water condenses on the inside of the tent and runs down to a collecting bottle. It can produce about 0.75 to 1 liter per day in calm conditions. However, rough conditions can cause the seawater in the bottom of the still to splash into the distilled water making it undrinkable.

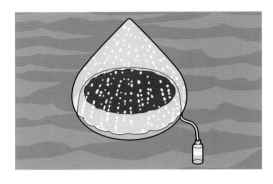

Hand-operated desalinator

Using reverse osmosis, a desalinator or water purifier pump will remove 98% of the salt from seawater. It can produce a little over 1 gallon (4 to 5 liters) of drinking water per hour but is hard physical work to operate. It may, in the heat of the day, cause the operator to sweat out more water than they can make. To make the most of a desalinator, use it at night when the weather is cooler.

Lone sailor Steve Callahan's yacht sank after a collision with a whale while on a transatlantic passage from the Canaries. He abandoned ship into his liferaft. In his grab bag were 8 pints of water and two solar stills. Seventy-six days and 1500 miles later he was picked up by fishermen within sight of land.

Bill and Simone Butler survived for 66 days in a liferaft by using a PUR Surviva 34 manual reverse-osmosis water filter after whales sank their 38ft yacht *Siboney* 1200 miles west of Panama.

What's on the menu

Catching food boosts survivors' emotional and physical well-being. Foods high in complex carbohydrates are more suitable than protein food such as meat and fish. Protein will draw water from the body while it is being digested. Ideally, the body needs just over a liter of water a day to digest food and dispose of waste matter. If no water is available, the survivor should not eat, as this will accelerate dehydration. If food is contained in the liferaft pack it will be high-energy carbohydrate, similar to a block of dried porridge.

- Plankton can be caught using an improvised net made from a pair of stockings or tights.

- Barnacles will grow on the bottom of the raft and the meat can be extracted and eaten.

- Fish can be caught using a harpoon, spear or gaff, or by hook and line.

An improvised spear can be formed by lashing a knife to a paddle. Steve Callahan included a spear gun in his grab bag, but if you do the same, take care not to puncture the raft.

Flying fish may also land on or in the raft.

Maurice and Maralyn Bailey adapted the safety pins in their first-aid kit to make fish hooks. On average, they landed forty fish a day.

Alain Bombard created hooks from a bone found just behind the gill of the Dorado fish.

Initially, lures can be made from silver paper. After that, most survivors have used the heads of the fish they caught as their bait. Poon Lim, who survived for 133 days on a lifeboat, used a dried paste of biscuit and saliva for his initial bait.

Fluid can be extracted from large fish by sucking their bones and eyes. The fish guts may be more digestible than the flesh.

Turtles—Dougal and Lyn Robertson and their family and crew caught turtles. Taking care that the creature's beak didn't damage their inflatable, they slit its throat and drank its blood immediately to rehydrate. The meat was dried and the blood used as a "sauce."

Seabirds—Poon Lim, Steve Callahan, and the Baileys all tell of catching and eating seabirds. Seagulls and boobys will often land on the liferaft or can be attracted by a baited hook.

Some form of chopping board is useful and can be improvised from the liferaft canister, flare box, or salvaged flotsam.

Keeping cool

While those in cold-water climates will be concerned about keeping warm, sailors in the tropics, are more concerned about staying cool and reducing dehydration caused by excessive sweating.

Methods of keeping cool

Obviously, stay under the canopy or create shade so that you can stay out of the sun. Rest during the heat of the day and undertake routine tasks in the morning and evening.

Cool the raft by wetting the canopy, and keep your clothes damp. Regularly rinse them in the sea to prevent a build-up of salt crystals, which would exacerbate sores.

In hot, calm weather, reattach the sea anchor to the entrance-side of the raft so that the wind blows into the raft.

During the day, deflate the inflatable floor and sit directly on the raft floor. Reinflate it at night to prevent getting cold.

If you are in a group of two or more rafts, spread the survivors equally between them so that each individual has more space to stretch.

Don't get into the water to cool down; you may not be able to get back into the raft.

CHAPTER 13 : Survival in cold water

Research by Golden and Hervey shows that the body goes through four stages when immersed in cold water:

Length of Time Immersed	Risks
0–3 minutes	Diving reflex and cold shock
3–30 minutes	Swim failure
More than 30 minutes	Hypothermia
Post-immersion	Hydrostatic squeeze, secondary drowning, post-rescue collapse (during and after rescue)

Because the human body loses heat 26 times faster in water than in air, immersion in cold water can be extremely dangerous. The graph below shows the possible effects of immersion in 50 degrees F water. Around the UK, sea temperature varies between 40 degrees F and 65 degrees F. The temperature of the Mediterranean during the summer rarely gets above 79 degrees F.

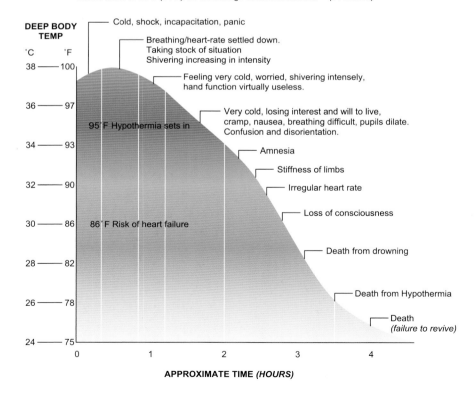

Typical change in deep body temperature during immersion in stirred water at 10˚C (50˚F) for an average clothed individual. *(F. Golden)*

Diving reflex

The diving reflex occurs when you first make contact with the water. If the water is not too cold you involuntarily hold your breath and your blood circulation and heartbeat slows. However, in water 60 degrees F and below, cold water shock may overcome the diving reflex.

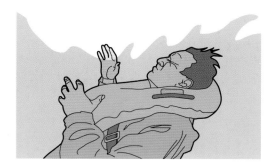

Cold shock

Cold shock takes place after thirty seconds to three minutes of immersion. Your breathing rate increases from around 10 breaths per minute to 60 breaths per minute (hyperventilation, which can cause dizziness and confusion). Breath-holding times are likely to reduce from over a minute to less than 10 seconds.

In water of less than 60 degrees F, it is probable that you will involuntarily inhale (gasp) even when underwater.

Blood vessels close to the skin shut down causing a sharp increase in blood pressure, which may be sufficient, depending on your fitness levels, to initiate a stroke or a heart attack.

Protecting against cold shock

To reduce the likelihood of cold shock, wear a lifejacket, waterproof clothing and, if possible, enter the water slowly. Do not try to swim—adopt the HELP position (see p.122).

Regular cold showers, baths or sea swimming can help to prepare your body for sudden immersion in cold water. Tests have shown that after just one week of daily cold showers, the effects of cold-water shock can be reduced by 50%.

The fitter you are, the better able you will be to withstand cold-water shock.

You are more likely to drown as a result of entering cold water quickly than you are from hypothermia.

Swim failure

After three to thirty minutes of being immersed in cold water, your arms and legs become numb and your muscles will not function properly. Shivering increases and your heart and breathing rate decreases.

Grip strength and coordination are significantly reduced. You may find it difficult to use your hands for firing flares, donning a spray hood, setting off a PLB or using a handheld VHF.

Even fit adult men can find it impossible to lift themselves up the side of a small boat and normally strong swimmers may only manage 100 yards before collapsing. This emphasizes the importance of wearing a lifejacket and being realistic about your swimming ability.

Hypothermia

Hypothermia can occur in water of up to 75 degrees F and sets in as the core body temperature drops from 98.6 to 95 degrees F. In northern European waters in the summer, your survival time with clothing and lifejacket is between two and twelve hours. In winter, it ranges from several minutes to two hours. The exact length of time depends upon on the water temperature, sea state, clothing, gender, fitness, health, shivering rate, and age of the person.

What happens?

The casualty will feel cold and their body becomes numb. Intense shivering may stop as the muscles become cramped and rigid. Speech will become slurred, nausea will set in and behavior will become irrational (similar symptoms to being drunk). The casualty will slip into unconsciousness, increasing their chances of drowning. Heart and breathing rates decrease and the pupils will dilate. Heart failure is possible when body temperature drops below 86 degrees F.

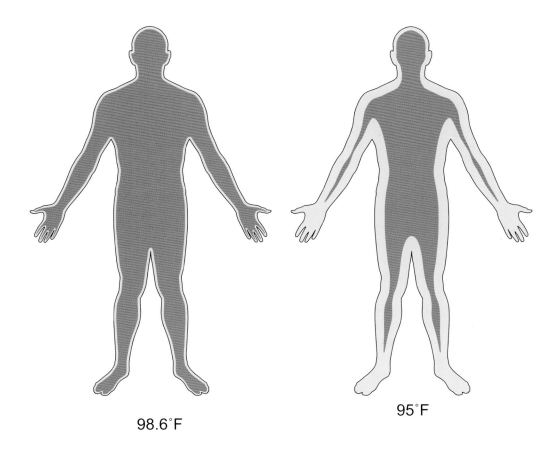

98.6°F

95°F

Methods to help prevent the onset of hypothermia

Before entering the water put on an immersion/survival suit, drysuit, wetsuit, or more clothing and a lifejacket.

Wear a hat and cover your head with a hood (this also makes you more visible to rescuers). Once in the water, do not kick off boots and try to remain as still as possible, adopting the HELP position (see fig. 1).

Get out of the water if at all possible.

Avoid alcohol.

Heat Escape Lessening Posture (HELP position)

A static body position reduces heat loss and increases your survival time. Therefore, assuming the HELP position is strongly recommended. However, holding this position may not be possible in anything other than calm conditions.

Lie with ankles crossed, knees together and legs slightly bent and elbows held close to the body with one hand under the front of the lifejacket. Hold the other hand up with the palm towards your face, covering the mouth and nose to protect the airway from waves and spray.

In wind and waves, a lifejacket wearer will be turned to face the waves, causing water and spray to break continually into their face. The natural reaction is to stabilize their position using their arms and legs and to turn their body so that the back of the head faces the waves.

A spray hood helps protect the face when both conscious and unconscious and is highly recommended. Put it on as soon as possible.

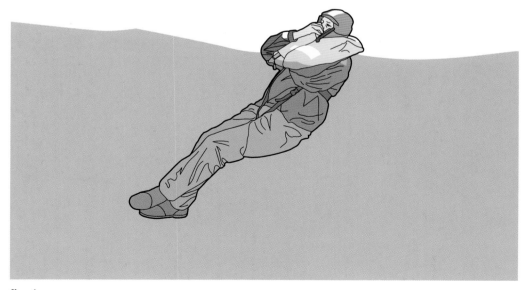

fig. 1

Swimming with a lifejacket

Avoid swimming if possible, since it increases heat loss, however if it is essential, swim on your back. Trying to swim on your front when wearing a lifejacket wastes energy. Swimming by kicking your legs loses less body heat than swimming with your arms but may not be as effective.

To reach other casualties, a liferaft or a survival craft in the water:

- Send a strong swimmer ahead, connected to the group by a line, or swim as a group.

- The "crocodile" may be used to swim as a group but it can be very difficult to achieve in waves.

- If a casualty is injured or unconscious, they should be placed at the tail of the crocodile.

Huddle

The huddle shares body heat, improves morale, supports weaker members of the group and increases your chances of being seen by rescuers. Use safety harnesses or rope to clip yourselves together as soon as possible, while your hands are still functional.

Be aware that in waves some members of the huddle will be facing wind and waves, making it impossible for them to hold their position.

Two person huddle—one person places their legs around the outside of the other. Take turns to be the person on the outside.

Group huddle—organize the group so that all use their right hand to hold on and their left hand to cover their airway or vice versa. Place injured or weak casualties in the middle of the huddle and rotate the huddle so that no one has to face wind and waves continuosly. Keep your ankles crossed and knees together to preserve body heat.

CHAPTER 14 : First aid

The quality of the first-aid kit supplied will vary depending on the quality of the liferaft. The SOLAS C first-aid kit provides a broad range of medical items and will be found on many rafts, or can be specified for inclusion.

The contents are shown below.

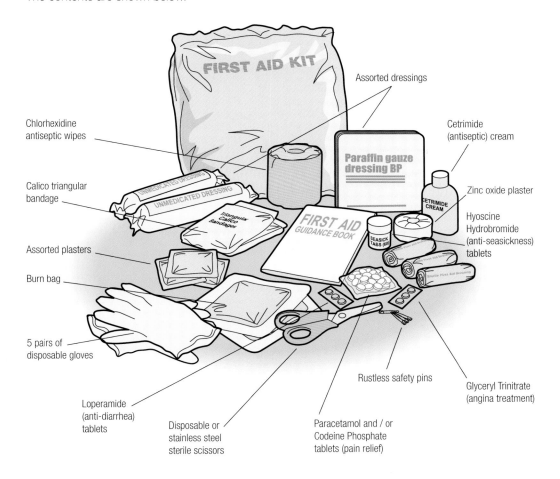

Assorted dressings

Chlorhexidine antiseptic wipes

Cetrimide (antiseptic) cream

Calico triangular bandage

Zinc oxide plaster

Hyoscine Hydrobromide (anti-seasickness) tablets

Assorted plasters

Burn bag

5 pairs of disposable gloves

Loperamide (anti-diarrhea) tablets

Disposable or stainless steel sterile scissors

Paracetamol and / or Codeine Phosphate tablets (pain relief)

Rustless safety pins

Glyceryl Trinitrate (angina treatment)

Not shown: Laerdal-type pocket mask (for expelled air resusitation)

In addition to conventional first-aid equipment, consider what else may be improvised. A lifejacket, for example, can be made into an inflatable splint to immobilize the lower leg, or alternatively, use two paddles or a plank of salvaged wood.

For general advice on diagnosis and treatment of casualties refer to the St. John's Ambulance First Aid Book (available from the RYA webshop). The RYA also has a one-day first-aid course for yachtsmen.

Heat exhaustion

This is a condition caused by the loss of water and salt from the body, usually as a result of physical exercise in a hot, moist environment.

Symptoms
Fatigue, headache, dizziness, nausea, possibly vomiting, and muscular cramps.

The skin will be cold, pale and clammy, the pulse weak and rapid, breathing fast and shallow.

Treatment
Remove the sufferer from direct heat and ventilate the liferaft. Sponge down their body, and give sips of cold water with a little salt.

Heat stroke

Caused by prolonged exposure to extreme heat or high humidity. The body temperature rises due to its inability to lose heat through sweating.

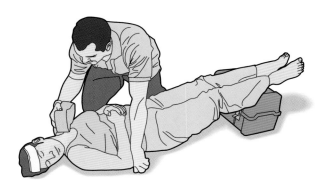

Symptoms
Similar to heat exhaustion except that the skin will look flushed and dry, the pulse is rapid and strong and breathing full and rapid.

Treatment
Sponge down the body, and give frequent sips of cool, slightly salted drinks. Help cool the sufferer by fanning or exposing them to a cooling breeze.

Hypothermia

You can become hypothermic in water of up to 75 degrees F. Around the UK, the water temperature varies between 40 degrees F and 65 degrees F. The temperature of the Mediterranean in the summer rarely rises above 78 degrees F.

Normal core body temperature is 98.6 degrees F. Hypothermia is defined to have occurred when the core temperature drops to 95 degrees F or below.

Hypothermia may occur in or out of the water. Liferaft occupants are susceptible due to the thin material insulating them from the cold water. Casualties that become cold relatively slowly—chronic hypothermia—such as those in a liferaft or those in water of temperatures between 68 and 82 degrees F will require different treatment from those who are suffering acute hypothermia from becoming cold quickly, such as falling into water below 59 degrees F.

Chronic hypothermic victims are more likely to be exhausted and unable to regain normal circulation on rewarming. Acute hypothermic casualties tend to respond well to rewarming and are soon back to normal.

Symptoms
The graph below shows the typical symptoms of a casualty who has fallen into 50-degree water as the body temperature falls.

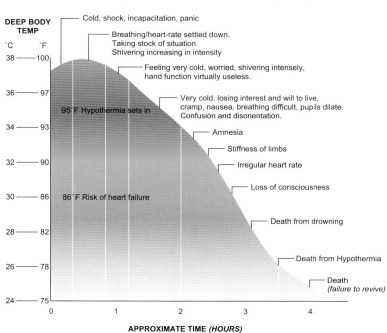

Typical change in deep body temperature during immersion in stirred water at 10°C (50°F) for an average clothed individual.   (F. Golden)

Without a thermometer it can be difficult to tell whether a person is cold or hypothermic. According to Golden and Tipton, one test is to feel the casualty's deep armpit; if it feels like cold marble, they are probably hypothermic.

Initially, the core temperature will rise as the blood vessels in the arms and legs contract, forcing blood back to the core. After the effects of cold-water shock have worn off, heart and breathing rates will slow and shivering will start and become more intense as the core temperature falls. Extremities become numb. Those in the water will suffer from swim failure as they become unable to control their limbs.

Speech will become slurred and the casualty may appear to be quiet and introverted. Nausea may be present and behavior may become irrational. They will lose coordination and become mentally slow. Chronic hypothermics will stop shivering as the body runs out of energy, and may suffer cramps. As cooling continues, the victim will become unconscious and, if in water without a lifejacket, will drown. In a raft, they will continue to cool, the heart and breathing rate will slow and pupils dilate. When their body temperature drops below 86 degrees F, they are in danger of heart failure.

Treatment

Hypothermia is difficult to treat in a survival situation. Passive rewarming is the suggested treatment. The aim is to stop further heat loss and give the body a chance to warm up from the inside.

If the casualty is conscious and cooperative, remove wet clothing. Insulate them with blankets and sleeping bags and wrap in plastic or a TPA. Leave the face exposed. Ensure the casualty is well insulated from the ground, deck or the floor of the raft. The body will slowly rewarm itself as the internal organs start to get back to normal.

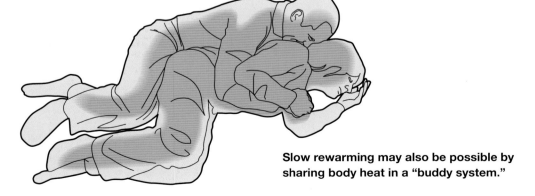

Slow rewarming may also be possible by sharing body heat in a "buddy system."

Warm drinks may be given to a conscious casualty. The hypothermic person can have lost as much as 2000 calories of heat.

DO NOT:
- Give alcohol
- Use hot-water bottles
- Massage/rub areas
- Handle roughly
- Administer fluid to a semi-/ unconscious person

Unconscious hypothermic casualties must be handled very carefully—otherwise they may collapse and die.

Active rewarming should only be undertaken by medical professionals. Even with the right knowledge, it is unlikely to be possible in a liferaft or small yacht.

Note: it can be difficult to tell if a hypothermic casualty's heart has stopped. Attempting CPR may fibrillate the heart and cause death.

The risk of drowning is reduced if you are wearing a good lifejacket with a spray hood.

Near-drowning

Symptoms
Breathing may have stopped or be very shallow; lips blue, bluish pallor of the face. Froth around the mouth, vomiting. If conscious, the patient may complain of chest pains and may be coughing.

Treatment
Use Expelled Air Resuscitation as soon as possible (see p.134). Water will be automatically coughed up from the lungs when breathing restarts. If available, apply oxygen. Seek further medical help.

Most diving boats carry oxygen and may be closer than medical services.

Secondary drowning

This occurs when a small amount of dirty water or seawater is inhaled into the lungs. A cupful is enough to do it. The water inflames the membranes of the lungs, which react by releasing fluid, filling the lungs thereby causing death by secondary drowning.

Symptoms
Increased chest pain and coughing (possibly with pink froth). Some people may show signs of asthma-type symptoms but many do not. It is likely to manifest itself up to 12 hours after the incident. Seek medical attention as soon as possible (and certainly before 12 hours) if you suspect a casualty has ingested water into the lungs.

Heart attack

Heart attack is always possible for those in a stressful situation. It is also a possible effect of cold-water shock and hypothermia. It is difficult to tell if a hypothermic casualty's heart is beating, if necessary, use CPR or an automatic heart defibrillator.

Symptoms
Vice-like central chest pain and pain in left or both arms that does not ease when the casualty rests; breathlessness, gasping for air, collapse, sudden dizziness, gray skin, sweating.

Treatment
Make the casualty as comfortable as possible, apply oxygen if available, give angina medicine (glyceryl trinitrate) and/or aspirin (300mg). Monitor and record vital signs. Seek medical advice.

Panic attack

Caused when the casualty has a sudden bout of extreme anxiety. This may be caused by the situation the casualty is in or brought on by symptoms caused by other illness. Either way, the effects on the casualty are very real and frightening.

Symptoms
Rapid breathing (hyperventilation) and a feeling of a racing heart beat. Muscular tension leading to headache, backache and a feeling of tightness across the chest. The casualty may believe they are dying and experience trembling, sweating and a dry mouth.

Treatment
If possible remove the cause of the fear. Reassure them and explain that they are having a panic attack. Get them to slow their breathing. If they are hyperventilating ask them to breathe into a paper bag (use an unused sick bag). Continue to reassure the casualty until they are recovered.

Shock

Caused by injury, burns, severe vomiting/diarrhea, fear, pain, or traumatic experience.

- The effect of shock must not be underestimated, it can be fatal. It is caused by reduced blood flow to the vital organs. Movement can cause fainting and even heart failure.

- Watch out for delayed shock. MOB casualties may say they are OK but may go into shock 20 to 60 minutes after recovery.

- Liferaft survivors are also susceptible—always check on quiet, introverted survivors, who may be suffering from shock.

Symptoms

Gray or pale skin that is cold but moist with sweat, feeling weak and faint, nausea, weak but rapid pulse, shallow breathing and perhaps gasping; thirst, possible unconsciousness.

Treatment

Most of the crew will have varying degrees of shock so there is little you can do in a liferaft.

Treat obvious wounds such as external bleeding and broken limbs. Lie the casualty down with their feet higher than their head. Loosen their clothing and if possible put them into the recovery position. Moisten lips with water. Do not apply hot water bottles.

If the casualty stops breathing commence ABC of resuscitation.

Severe bleeding

External bleeding is obvious and distressing, and can lead to shock. The aims are to stem the flow and minimize the chances of infection.

Treatment
Cover the wound with a dressing and apply direct pressure. Raise the wound to reduce blood loss, and bandage the area. Keep applying dressings until the bleeding stops. Support the injury. If an object is embedded in the wound, do not remove it. Provide padding either side of object. Apply dressings.

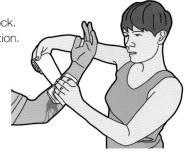

Frostbite

On watch, crew may be in danger of frostbite, where local tissue becomes frozen. The areas affected are usually the fingers, toes, ears or nose. Prevention is better than cure. Wear gloves, cover the face and ears and to be aware of the length of watch duties. Exercise and massage can delay the onset of cold injury.

Symptoms
The area becomes pale then white, mottled blue and finally bluish black; there is swelling and fluid release from damaged cells and loss of feeling.

Treatment
Remove constricting garments, raise and dry the affected area. Warm the hands or feet by putting them under the armpits, in the groin or between another person's hands.

Do not massage or burst blisters or apply pressure.

Immersion foot

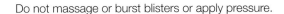

Known during World War One as Trench Foot, immersion foot is caused by continuous contact with a cold and wet environment.

Symptoms
Feet become white as local circulation is reduced, causing swelling of tissues and numbness.

Treatment
Dry feet, use rapid rewarming, encourage gentle exercise and, if possible, give warm drinks.

As the foot warms, it will become painful.

Fractures and dislocations

Broken bones can be either open or closed fractures. If it is an open fracture, treat as for bleeding (p.132) and then immobilize the affected limb. If it is a closed fracture or a dislocation, the broad aim is to immobilize the limb to make it more comfortable.

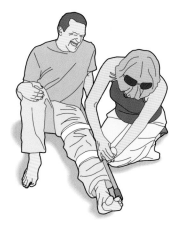

For leg fractures, the leg can be immobilized by improvising a splint from paddles and bandages, rope, or strapping.

A lifejacket can be used to immobilize the lower leg. Place the ankle into the neck of the lifejacket with the lifejacket's body either side of the calf. Wrap it gently over the leg and apply strapping at the top, middle and bottom. Gently inflate the jacket by mouth until it is firm.

Seasickness

Seasickness is a debilitating illness that comes on rapidly, especially in the confines of a liferaft, at a time when the crew need to be as alert and able as they can be. If possible, take anti-seasickness medication before entering the raft or as soon as possible after boarding the raft.

Symptoms
Nausea and vomiting, pale clammy skin. Wishing never to go afloat again!

Treatment
Take anti-seasickness medication in the form of hyoscine hydrobromide. If vomiting has already started there is little point in taking more, because they are unlikely to be ingested. It's also possible that, if all the tablets are kept down, serious side effects will be experienced. Side effects can be drowsiness, dry mouth and blurred vision. Excessive doses of seasickness pills can produce hallucinations.

Do not attempt cardiac massage in a raft unless it has a wooden floor.

Resuscitation technique

Before attempting resuscitation, make the following checks:

1. Is the casualty responding to you?

If not, check the airway for breathing.

2. Look at the casualty's chest. Is it moving?

If not, tilt the head back to open the casualty's airway.
Check and remove any obstructions in the mouth.

Listen at the casualty's mouth for sounds of breathing. Hold your cheek close to their nose and mouth and feel for warm air movement. Alternatively, condensation forming on a cold mirror or metal spoon held close to their mouth and nose can also indicate breathing.

It is now accepted that if breathing is not present, circulation is not present either and that resuscitation should now be attempted. It is assumed that the casualty has suffered a cardiac arrest.

Place the heel of your hand in the center of their chest.
Place the heel of your other hand on top of the first hand.
Interlock the fingers. Do not apply pressure over the upper abdomen or the bottom end of the breastbone (sternum).

Apply 30 chest compressions at the rate of 100 per minute.

Tilt the head back by placing a finger under the chin to open the casualty's airway. Allow the mouth to open but maintain chin lift.

Place your mouth over casualty's mouth to achieve a good seal and blow into mouth.

Watch for the chest rising. Remove your mouth and allow the chest to fall.

Repeat the rescue breath. Start chest compressions again.

For non-drowning—generally cardiac arrest—casualties, give 30 chest compressions to two chest compressions.

For suspected drowning casualties: Check for breathing as for cardiac arrest. If not apparent, give five rescue breaths followed by one minute of chest compressions, continue until help arrives.

Pre-rescue collapse

Hypothermic casualties can suffer collapse at the thought of imminent rescue. Although not proven, it's believed that the feeling of overwhelming relief causes chemical changes within the body, which suddenly reduces blood pressure and so causes the casualty to collapse.

Circum-rescue collapse and hydrostatic squeeze

A combination of hypothermia with the sudden onset of physical action can result in some survivors collapsing and dying while being rescued.

Immersed casualties are at higher risk. In addition to the effects of hypothermia, water pressure on the lower limbs squeezes blood flow back into the body and is helping to support circulation.

When the casualty is lifted vertically from the water, the full effect of gravity creates extra strain on the heart. This may lead to unconsciousness or even death.

Immersed and hypothermic casualties should be treated with great care. If recovering from water they should be lifted horizontally to minimize the gravitational effects on the heart.

Post-rescue

Survivors are not survivors until they have survived.

Even after rescue there is a chance that the survivor will succumb to the effects of their ordeal.

This can be due to secondary drowning. Even those that show no immediate signs of aspirating seawater should be regularly checked during the hours immediately after immersion.

Rewarming survivors too quickly may result in a catastrophic drop in blood pressure. Active rewarming needs to be monitored professionally. Take care when taking hypothermic survivors into a warm cabin. Avoid warming by a shower or hot bath unless monitored by a medical professional.

Internal bleeding caused when the casualty fell into the water may not be obvious when a hypothermic MOB is recovered. If the MOB fell heavily, they should be monitored while the body rewarms. Seek medical advice.

CHAPTER 15 : Life-saving signals

These signals are used by ships, aircraft, or persons in distress to communicate with rescue service stations, lifeboats, vessels and aircraft engaged in search-and-rescue operations. Use the most suitable signal for the situation and taking into account the prevailing conditions.

Search-and-rescue unit replies

These indicate that you have been seen and assistance will be given as soon as possible.

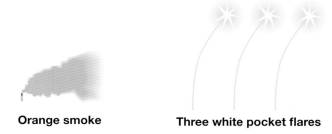

Orange smoke **Three white pocket flares**

Surface-to-air signals

These are shown by means of lights or flags or by laying out the symbol on the ground or deck in highly contrasting colors.

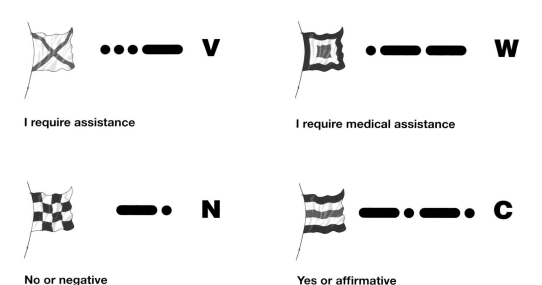

I require assistance **I require medical assistance**

No or negative **Yes or affirmative**

Air-to-surface direction signals

Sequence of three maneuvers meaning **"Go in this direction**." May be used to show which way to go to assist another vessel or to indicate direction to a safe haven.

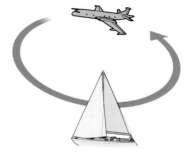

1. plane circles vessel at least once

2. plane crosses low, ahead of boat, rocking wings

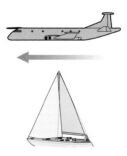

3. plane flies over boat in the direction to go

Your assistance is no longer required

Plane crosses low, astern of vessel, rocking wings

Shore-to-ship signals

Safe to land here
Vertical waving of arms, white flag, light or flare.
Morse code letter K—dah dit dah

K –

Landing here is dangerous with additional signals that indicate direction of safer landing place

Horizontal waving of white flag, light or flare.

Go this way

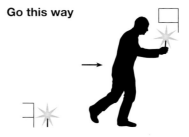

Putting one flag or flare on ground and moving in direction of safer landing area with the other indicates direction of safer landing

May also be shown by Morse code light or sound

S— ●●● = landing here is dangerous

R— ●━● = land to the right of your current heading

L— ●━●● = land to the left of your current heading

Air-to-surface replies

Message understood

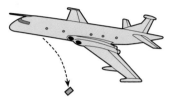

Drop a message

or rocking wings

or flashing landing lights on and off twice

T **R**

or Morse code by light T = dah or R = dit dah dit

Message not understood

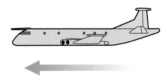

Straight and level flight

or Circling

Or Morse code by light R P T

R **P** **T**

Surface-to-air replies

Message understood—I will comply
Change course to required direction
Or Morse code by light T = ⬛ or code and answering pendant

I am unable to comply
Morse code by light N = ⬛● or code flag N

CHAPTER 16 : Rescue

Make yourself as visible as possible. An EPIRB will tell the SAR authorities where you are and who you are. But it's wise not to rely on any one system.

You will see potential rescuers before they see you. Try to make contact with them. Use flares only when there's a chance of rescuers seeing them. Use a handheld VHF and / or a signaling miror.

But be prepared for disappointment. A common theme of all survival stories is that they could have been rescued earlier if only the passing ship had seen them.

Don't celebrate early—they may not be able to pick you up and you might have to wait a few more hours. You haven't been rescued until you are safely on board the ship or helicopter.

Rescue by lifeboat

If rescued by lifeboat, you'll probably see the boat searching for you before they see you. Use a handheld flare to help pinpoint your position.

If it's dark, switch on the liferaft light and use a torch to signal to them. Talk to them on a handheld VHF—they will use their direction finder to home in on you—but help confirm their bearing by telling them where you are using a hand held GPS or relative to their direction of travel. Use nautical terms. "I am on your port bow, half a mile…" etc.

Tell them if you have injured casualties or children and the condition of the survivors. This will help the coxswain make the best plan for their evacuation. Tell them if there are any ropes or hazards around the raft—it may affect their approach.

As the lifeboat approaches, show the crew that you have a painter—assuming you cut it at the correct point when abandoning ship. The crew will then be able to secure the raft alongside during the rescue. If they throw you a heaving line, find a strongpoint and attach it—you will not have the strength to hold it while they pull the raft in.

The lifeboat will approach either head- or stern-to-wind to avoid becoming entangled in the sea anchor or other loose lines.

Rescue by ship

While many professional ships' crews practice emergency recovery, there are some that may have no idea how to go about retrieving survivors from a small boat or liferaft.

It's important to communicate effectively with them because it will be difficult for the captain and crew to appreciate the size and effects of the waves on a small vessel or liferaft.

Beware—the liferaft (or boat) can be sucked in to a lightly loaded ship's propellers.

Due to exhaustion and the effects of the cold, you will not be in a fit state to climb a ship's ladder. In the excitement of the rescue, it's easy to think you can. There are many reported cases where survivors have tried to climb the ladder only to be lost when they fall off it after climbing only a few rungs.

The ship may be able to lower a basket or a cargo net to lift everyone in together. A large net can lift the whole raft with the survivors inside.

The best option is for the ship to lower a fast rescue craft that will come to the raft and pick up survivors. The ship will stand off and create a lee for the rescue boat to work. The rescue craft, its crew and the survivors will then be lifted back on board. This avoids exerting the survivors. Remember to take your small grab bag with ID documents, etc.

> Hypothermic casualties should lie down in the rescue boat with their heads towards the stern of the boat.

Rescue by helicopter

As with lifeboat rescue, the helicopter may have difficulty seeing you. If a 406/121.5 EPIRB or PLB is available, make sure it's switched on and operating. Switch on the liferaft lights—they may seem dim to you but a pilot using night-vision goggles will see them clearly, use your torch to signal to the helicopter.

If you have one, use a handheld VHF to communicate with the helicopter. Pilots use clock notation. For example, "We are lying at your 4 o'clock."

Use orange smoke—during the day—or handheld red flares to pinpoint your position.

Do not fire parachute rocket flares if the helicopter is within a short distance.

A rocket flare has the capability to down a helicopter.

At night, a bright flare can blind a pilot wearing night-vision goggles. If in radio contact, ask before firing a hand-held flare. It probably will not be necessary.

The helicopter crew will instruct you what to do. Do as they say—they are the experts.

Take care not to all crowd to one side of the raft or dinghy—the prevailing wind and the downdraught of the helicopter may be enough to turn the raft over.

Most SAR helicopters will lower a winch man into the raft. Be aware that some countries' SAR units use different methods. Some may drop a rescue diver first, others may use a rescue basket.

> Helicopters quickly build a charge of static electricity. Do not grab the winch man until he has "earthed" into the water.

If the helicopter is using a "hi-line" to help guide and steady the winch man, hold on to the line while the winch man is pulled back up to the helicopter. Do not tie it to the raft, and make sure it does not become tangled with the remaining casualties.

Hi-line

Hi-line

If the winch man suspects a casualty is hypothermic he will lift them in a horizontal position either in a stretcher or use a double strop—one underneath the arms and one under the back of the knees.

GLOSSARY

bear away	turn the boat downwind
bilge pump	pump for removing water from inside hull
bow thruster	an impellor mounted sideways in a tube below the waterline in the bow to assist maneuvering
cleat	a fitting to which ropes are attached
coachroof	cabin roof
cold-water shock	physiological reaction to immersion in cold water
companionway	entrance to cabin, generally down steps
dan buoy	highly visible float thrown to a man overboard
datum point	marked position on which sector search is based
diving reflex	involuntary breathing reaction when falling into cold water
drogue	funnel shaped canvas device trailed from stern to help prevent craft from slewing sideways in following sea
DSC	Digital Selective Calling—automated VHF radio facility
EDR	Expected Detection Range
EPIRB	Emergency Position Indicating Radio Beacon—satellite-based location system
fairlead	metal fitting used to guide rope
fulcrum	pivot point
GMDSS	Global Maritime Distress and Safety System
GPS	Global Positioning System—satellite-based navigation system
grab bag	watertight buoyant bag for stowing essential items for emergency use
Granny bar	crew support bar around mast
gunwale	top edge of hull

halyard	rope for raising or lowering sail
handybilly	block and tackle
heaving to	bring boat to a standstill
heliograph	signalling system using mirror to reflect sun's rays
HELP position	Heat Escape Lessening Posture—position adopted in water
"hi-line"	winching technique used by SAR helicopters
HRU (hydrostatic release unit)	device triggered by immersion in water
hydrostatic squeeze	condition where water pressure on lower limbs squeezing blood back into body is removed, thereby placing strain on the heart
hypothermia	condition of having body temperature reduced to dangerously low level
immersion foot	condition caused by continuous contact with cold and wet environment
immersion suit	waterproof insulated emergency survival suit
ISAF	International Sailing Federation
ISO	International Standards Organization
jackstay	line at deck level for attaching lifelines
jury-rig	makeshift repair, e.g. to sails or steering
kicker	control pulling boom downwards (also vang)
leeward	downwind direction
luffing	heading into wind
Mayday call	distress call
MMSI number	Maritime Mobile Service Identities number
MOB	man overboard

moment of inertia	force of rotation of boat dependent on weight of mast, keel etc.
ORC	Offshore Racing Congress
painter	mooring line attached to dinghy or liferaft
Pan Pan call	radio call seeking assistance
parbuckle	sling of canvas or rope used for raising objects
PEPIRB	Personal Emergency Position Indicating Radio Beacon—satellite-based location system (see PLB)
pitch-poling	capsizing with bow going over stern
PLB	Personal Locator Beacon—satellite-based or surface-based emergency location system
PRV	pressure-relief valve
reefing pennant	rope used to assist in reducing sail
RNLI	Royal National Lifeboat Institution
roller headsail	sail in front of mast set or reduced from a roller device
SAR	search and rescue
SART	Search-and-Rescue Radar Transponder—alert and position-finding electronic device
scandalize the boom	raise the outer end of the boom
sea anchor	parachute-like device deployed from bow to keep head-to-wind and reduce possibility of capsize or pitch-poling
seacock	valve in hull controlling seawater flow into boat
secondary drowning	physiological reaction caused by presence of water in lungs
Senhouse slip	release attachment for straps, etc.
shrouds	wires holding up the mast at sides of boat

signal card	card showing meanings of signals from ships and aircraft
snap shackle	fitting allowing quick attachment/removal of rope
solar still	solar-operated device for extracting potable water from seawater
SOLAS	Safety of Life at Sea Convention
sponson	inflated hull section of inflatable craft
spreaders	mast fittings guiding rigging from hull to mast head
stanchion	post supporting guardrail
steerage	steering effectiveness dependent on flow of water past rudder
storm jib	small sail set before mast for storm conditions
strum box	bilge pump filter
tack	change direction by bringing the wind around the front of the boat
topping lift	rope that holds the boom up when the sail is down
TPA	thermal protective aid—insulated bag-like suit for casualties
trysail	small loose-footed sail set in place of mainsail for storm conditions
turnbuckle	device for adjusting tension in rigging
vang	control pulling boom downwards (also kicker)
warp	mooring line
washboard	removable board at top of companionway to minimize ingress of water into cabin
Williamson turn	maneuver by powered craft to turn onto reciprocal track

INDEX